MARRIAGE IS SUPPOSED TO BE FOREVER

BY

REV. CAREY N. INGRAM

Copyright © 2001 by Rev. Carey N. Ingram

Published by
Orman Press Inc.
4200 Sandy Lake Drive
Lithonia, GA 30038

ISBN 1-891773-23-2

All Rights Reserved. No part of this book may be used or reproduced in any form or by any means, including photocopying, without the written permission from the publisher.

DEDICATION

This book is dedicated to my dear wife, Judy,
my earthly inspiration, and to
my children, Tashia, Joshua, and Michelle,
my pride and joy.

SPECIAL THANKS & ACKNOWLEDGEMENTS

None of us can do anything all by ourselves; and when it comes to the things I try to do, I owe so many. I want to first of all thank the Lord for giving me the vision and courage to step up to the plate and get this done. With God, all things are possible. I want to give thanks to Judy, who would on occasions remind me to stop and relax by writing on my book. It paid off. Mrs. Janice B. Wright edited my work. She truly made the rough edges smooth without compromising my style and colloquialism. Thanks Sister Janice for your labor of love and patience.

To my staff: my business manager and consultant, Ms. Lisa Jones, and little Doug, her assistant; Mrs. April Wells and Nyresha. Thanks to my lawyer, Mr. Chris Tywman, for his legal services and advice; and to the church secretary, Ms. Terri Haynes, who always helps me with these extra projects.

Special thanks to the 100 Black Men of Rome, Inc., who purchased a large number of books to place in our schools libraries. Mr. Alvin Jackson who underwrote this book so I would not be worried about it's financing. I could not have done this without you, Alvin. I want to thank Mr. Tommy Williams of 96 South Carolina for his artistic drawing of my concept for the book cover. Last, but not least, thanks to the Lovejoy Church Family for believing in me and encouraging me to be all I can be... all to the glory of God!!!

I want to remember my mentors who are as much a part of this project as anyone, for when I speak, so do they. My grandmother, Mrs. Marie Maddox, Rev. Dr. O. B. Yates, the late Rev. Dr. O. M. Collins, Deacon Sam Burrell, the late Deacon "Dee" Evins Oliver, and the late Rev. Curtis Moreland who told me, "Talk, talk, talk, is cheap, cheap, cheap... Do, do, do, and you will, will, will."

Table of Contents

Foreword...VII

Introduction..IX

Chapter One..1
IF You Want the Right One, Be the Right One

Chapter Two...13
Understanding Just What Marriage Is

Chapter Three..23
Keep the Lines of Communication Open

Chapter Four...33
Duties of the Husband and Wife

Chapter Five..43
Be Aware of Family and Friends

Chapter Six..53
Family Values

Chapter Seven...61
The Power of Planning

Chapter Eight..71
My Wife's Perspective

Chapter Nine...79
Fidelity, the Art of Being Trusted

Chapter Ten..89
Marriage is Supposed to be Forever

About the Author..99

FOREWORD

We cannot over emphasize the importance of positive home and family life. In the final analysis, the strength of our nation has its origin in our home and families. The primary source of moral, spiritual and ethical training should begin at home.

School, governmental agencies and churches should not be left entirely with the task of raising children. Let me hasten to say that they do in fact have significant roles in the upbringing of children, however, they cannot do it all. Parents cannot escape their responsibilities for rearing their own children.

There is growing evidence of various kinds that would very strongly suggest that home and family life, as we once knew it, is in a state of decline. Data from numerous sources would indicate that there is much work to be done in strengthening our homes. This problem, as we see it, would collectively address itself to society as a whole. We cannot afford to stand idly by and watch the very foundation of our society (home/family) gradually but surely erode away. Hopefully this treatise will provide some specific thing we can do to bring about a new direction in our homes.

There is an often repeated statement which we hear many, many times and it is spoken thus: "If the United States Supreme Court had not ruled out prayer in schools, everything would be all right."

On the other hand however, the court did not say we could not pray in our homes. God must necessarily be firmly re-established in our homes. Growing numbers of young people are exiting homes that are indeed godless and fatherless. This does not necessarily mean that there is no place for them in an organized society. It is our duty, however, to assist them with their development as responsible citizens. Conversely, our human and other resources are really extended as we attempt to successfully meet the needs of a number of these individuals. Again, the process of assisting young people with their development into responsible men and women is a long and tedious process.

There is an ancient adage, which reads as follows: When there is trouble in the home–there is trouble in the state. When there is trouble in the state–there is trouble in the nation. When there is trouble in the nation–there is trouble in the world. These statements would appear to point to our homes as being the foundation of our strength as a society.

In conclusion, marriage was ordained by God. Marriage is the gateway to wholesome home and family life. Any union of men and women outside the bonds of marriage is a direct violation of God's moral laws. The sanctity of our homes must be preserved. Historical facts will show that some of our greatest civilizations in the past have crumbled into the dust of the earth when God's moral laws are not honored. Their demise began with a weakening of home and family life.

—Samuel T. Burrell

Mr. Burrell is a retired teacher and school administrator of the Rome City School System, where he served for over 40 years. He has served as a Deacon, Sunday School Teacher, Bible Class Teacher, and Treasurer at his church. He and his wife, Josephine, have been married for over 50 years.

INTRODUCTION

A Perfect Wedding

It was without a doubt the largest and most beautiful wedding I have ever seen. As a minister, I have officiated many wedding ceremonies. Several of these weddings were very impressive; but not in my 20 plus years in ministry have I witnessed such a wedding as the one on July 25, 1998. It was the wedding ceremony of our dear friend Angela Maria Kidd and Rev. Darren Bernard Vinson.

Now this couple has been married just a little more than 3 years, and if I were a betting man (and I am not), I sure would bet that Angela and Darren will live happily ever after. I certainly am pulling for them. Let me share with you why I believe this marriage stands a good chance of survival.

First of all, whereas we (my wife, Judy and I) didn't know Darren, Angela had been a dear friend for many years. She once worked here in Rome as a school teacher. She and Judy worked at the same elementary school. They became good friends and in a short period of time, Angela was a regular in attendance at our church. We knew she loved the Lord. We also knew that she was serious about marriage, even to the point of not getting married if she did not find a man who met her criteria as a godly man. He did not have to be a preacher, but he certainly had to love the Lord.

Angela was a confident and mature young lady. On more than one occasion when my wife and I took trips out of town, we left our children with Angela. We knew she possessed the qualities needed to handle teenagers. It was always my belief that she would someday find that special gentleman for the special lady she was.

Angela moved back to her home town of Athens, Georgia, a few years ago, and we kept in touch. One day in March of 1998 (and it seemed out of the clear blue sky because Angela had not mentioned at any other time a fella in her life), she sent us a wedding invitation. When she introduced her fiancee as Rev. Darren Vinson, we felt like Angela had picked the right one.

After all (it is a fact), people who share strong values and a belief system tend to do well. People who believe in God through Christ increase their chance of having a faithful and happy marriage. The latest statistics on marriages tell us 8 out of 10 end in divorce. Yet only 1 out of 1,000 marriages of born again Christians end in divorce. Yes, I believe Angela and Darren have an excellent chance of making their union an enduring and blissful relationship.

We believed this so much that we got up early one Saturday in July and headed for the Ebenezer Baptist Church in West Athens. We knew it would be something special, because we knew Angela. But neither our hearts nor our minds were ready for what we witnessed that day.

This wedding was awesome. Historic Ebenezer Baptist Church had probably never seen this kind of crowd in years. The 800 seat sanctuary was overflowing. The church parking lot and streets on either side of the church for blocks were a sign that on this day this wedding was the place to be. There was a magic in the air. Everyone was excited.

When we got to the church and saw how the crowd was gathering, I found myself panicking to find a parking place. Once we found a place to park the car, Judy, Michelle (our baby girl), and I found ourselves in a fast walk (almost a jog) trying to get to the church to get a seat because we didn't want to miss anything.

For one of the few times in my life, I was at a wedding and nobody offered Judy and me special treatment. It was every person for himself to get a seat. I kept telling ushers and others that I was Rev. Ingram from Rome, Ga., and a friend of the family. They smiled but offered no special place for us. We did get seats. They were in the back on the right side of the middle isle. It was a good view. I simply wanted to be up closer, and all of a sudden I wanted to be more involved. It was like royalty was getting married. And as children of God, they were royalty.

People from across racial, denominational, and class lines participated and were in attendance. More than 1,000 people came from all across the country to let Angela and Vinson know how happy they were for them, and to witness what even Mr. Kidd (Angela's dad) had declared "the wedding I thought would never take place."

I don't recall if I heard bells ringing, but bells were ringing in all of our hearts. Then the ceremony began. I have often said that every wedding ceremony has its own personality, and this wedding took on the personality of sacred worship. On the cover of the wedding program was a picture of a Bible opened to these words: "I have found the one whom my soul loves ..." (Song of Solomon).

Angela and Darren had been careful to include everyone, it seems. There were two officiating Ministers. Reverend Dr. Windred Hope prayed and gave amazingly unique and timely illustrations to define what it meant to be married. Reverend Marvin Simmons led them through the exchange of vows and rings, and did the pronouncement of marriage. He carried out this wedding in such a way as to invoke low volume, yet firm "Amens." Trust me, Angela and Darren were married. There was a maid of honor and a best man, flower girls and a ring bearer, twelve groomsmen and bridesmaids each. This wedding had a full choir, and they sang wedding hymns, anthems, and Gospel songs (like on Sunday Morning).

Several times I came close to getting up and clapping my hands to the presence of the Lord, and I was not alone. When Darren shared his vows with Angela, he not only held her hand, it seemed as if he was holding her. When Angela said her vows, she cried and Darren held her closer. It was simply heavenly. It was one of those rare moments that we all have in our lives when we truly experience a sacred, spiritual uplifting that speaks to our hearts and says, "all is well." It was something that money can't buy. You couldn't produce the effect again if you tried. It was not a ceremony that we observed but rather, it was a worship service that possessed us. On the back of the program were these words:

To our family and friends:

The test of our love for one another is the love we have for our Lord.

Thank you for your prayers and your love and for witnessing our vows to each other and to our Creator.

Angela and Darren

To sum it up, this was a great wedding experience. Judy, Michelle, and I voted this wedding as the wedding of the century. This ceremony took us somewhere and gave us hope. But marriage is more than the wedding day and honeymoon. Marriage is supposed to be forever.

It was Darren and Angela's wedding that set things in motion. I began to think about my own marriage.

As I write these words I am less than a year away from celebrating my Silver Anniversary (25 years) with Judy. It might sound like a cliché but it doesn't seem like 25 years. And as I reminisce about those years, the thing that stands out most is that they have been happy years. Maybe that's because I choose not to remember those trying and difficult periods at certain intervals in my marriage, which now seem like only a few days, hours, and minutes. The bad days or the tough times, as I think back, are just not to be compared to thousands of days and hours that were really great. So as I think of my faithful marriage, I also see it as a successful marriage, because we're still in love and we're still having fun. We believe that the best is yet to come.

When I think of the 60 plus weddings that I have performed and the hundreds of hours I've spent counseling and encouraging people, I am inspired to share the information that God and my life experiences have taught me on this very important subject. So these words come from my perspective; a man married for almost 25 years, a country preacher who believes marriages should be divinely inspired. In almost every point I make, I will share scripture as a point of reference to what I believe God is saying about relationships.

It is my sincere belief that I have something to offer the reader of this little book. I believe that the key to turning around a society that is declining in its morale and morals is to give people an injection of hope into the oldest institution on the earth (Genesis 2:24)–The Marriage Institute. I am a witness that in the midst of all the temptations of this alluring, intriguing, and extraordinary world, if a man and woman want to, together they can work through, overcome, and conquer the obstacles that will surely come their way. After all, marriage is supposed to be forever.

CHAPTER ONE

IF You Want the Right One, Be the Right One

Rev. Dr. Jasper Williams, Pastor of the Salem Baptist Church in Atlanta, Georgia, raised this question in a sermon: "How do you know if the person you are dating is the right one for you to marry?" He answered the question with this statement: "If you want the right one, be the right one," and to me that is so true. I am convinced that a person who is looking for a real relationship with someone should first of all know himself or herself.

Let me raise these questions for your consideration. What are the things you like? What are some things you love? What are some things you dislike? What is it that you simply will not tolerate in your life? What's really important to you? Do you know your capabilities and limitations? What is your desired vocation? What do you want to be doing five or maybe ten years from now? Where do you want to live? Have you come up with a plan to reach your goals? Are you willing to pay the price of hard work, sacrifice, and commitment to get what you want out of life?

Before you consider another person sharing your life, questions like these must be addressed. This is your life, and you must have some stability before you involve someone else. So the first step in a relationship with another is for you to make sure that you know who you are. Perhaps then you can determine who it is (or at least the qualities and character of the person) you would want to share your life with. 2 Corinthians 6:14 declares, "Be ye not unequally yoked together with unbelievers: for what fellowship hath righteousness with unrighteousness? and what communion hath light with darkness?"

Judy and I share a very unique situation because we have known each other all our lives and were childhood sweethearts. We grew up in the housing projects. At first, she dreaded the times she saw me turn a corner because she said I was always being mannish and a smart mouth.

Yet, we already had some things in common. We both lived in the housing projects and were without dads, and we knew what it was like not to get things you wanted. We were both the babies of our families, so we both were spoiled to some extent. As we grew into adolescence we became friends, and because of some common things in our background, we often shared what we wanted in life and how we planned to get where we wanted to be.

By the time I was a senior in high school and Judy a sophomore, we considered ourselves boyfriend and girlfriend, and this with our parents' approval. This relationship was strictly friendship. I was ready for anything I could get away with, but Judy knew how to keep me at arm's length. I quickly learned to respect her for the stand she took about who she was and what she wanted to do with her life. We were close friends who genuinely cared about each other, looked out for each other, and did a lot of things together. Living in the housing projects, we saw a lot of poverty, ignorance, teenage pregnancies, crime and bitterness. In a sense, we gave each other hope.

I was two years older than Judy and an outgoing and aggressive guy. Judy was passive and shy. I talked all the time–a loud mouth–often doing dumb things just for attention. Judy was not a public kind of person. She had her family and a small circle of girlfriends, and otherwise kept to herself. I was a basketball player; she was a basketball cheerleader. We had some things in common, yet we were two very different people with two very different personalities.

Our families moved out of the housing projects as we were growing into adolescence. I lived with my grandparents whose home was next door to a church–the Springfield Baptist Church–that would change my life forever.

Almost immediately, church became a very meaningful part of my life. You know how that goes: I was a stinker, but grandma insisted that I go to church. So every Sunday, I mean every Sunday, we had to go to church. The church then became not only a place of worship, but also a place of socializing, meeting friends, being creative, and a place of discovery. For example, I was always interested in singing and being in dramatic or musical plays. Often, I would write a play and we'd perform it at church. I enjoyed singing and our church's youth choir was considered among the best in town, or at least we thought so. This led to citywide choirs and trips out of town to sing. As I grew in these church affairs, naturally I included Judy. It wasn't long before she moved her membership to Springfield and our relationship grew. Now, we were growing more and more as friends and growing in Christ. I'm so glad we were teenagers growing up as Christians. I certainly had some personal problems, but I had a basic understanding about God. This gave me stability.

    I was a Christian and I loved the Lord, but I was also a young man with my hormones kicking. I was not a virgin, so I knew what it was like to be with a girl. My problem was I simply had not been with the one that I felt like I was in love with. I was aggressive, and these were difficult days for Judy and me because by now we were touching. (If you don't want to get in too deep with your girlfriend or boyfriend, you had better not do a lot of touching.) I must confess it was Judy's willpower and the grace of God that kept us, I had nothing to do with it. I kept trying to assure her that I was going to marry her and that as far as I was concerned, we were already married and could go with the feelings. We had some other problems too, like my roving eyes. I wanted to go, go, and go. She was more of a hang-around-the-house and neighborhood person. I was older and had other interests. She seemed really into her family and school. We were different, but I'm convinced that we genuinely loved each other for as much as what we understood love to be, and I'll tell you more about that later. But we were definitely friends with common ideas, dreams, and aspirations. We often wondered if we could fulfill those ideas, dreams, and aspirations together.

    The only college I got accepted to was Shorter College right in my hometown, and that was just fine because by this time I really did not want to be separated from Judy. I knew by the end of my freshman year in college that I was going to marry her. At the end of my junior year and her freshman year in college, we were married. (I wanted the right one, so I had to be the right one.) And by this time, I had settled down.

If you're going to be the right one, you must keep yourself pure. Now I am sorry and asked God to forgive me for the times in my life when I allowed my lustful nature to lead me to sin. However, I reaped what I sowed in that I brought a lot of unnecessary baggage into my marriage. I brought a lot of petty jealousies, insecurities, and unfair expectations. This was due in part to the fact that my life was clouded with past indiscretions. I had not been trustworthy, so I didn't trust. I had told lie after lie, so I didn't believe others when they talked to me. I was angry because I had not fully prepared for the transition from college to the work force. Guess who I had a tendency to take that out on? But thank God I changed. I grew up, I matured. And if I can change, anybody can change. If you are looking to be the right one, then don't be afraid to change.

A man talked about a letter his daughter wrote him while in college. "Dad, when I see how casual most of my friends are about having sex, they make it seem so natural and inevitable. It makes me wonder, what am I waiting for?" Dad's reply: "I think I can tell you what you are waiting for, you are waiting to be free. Free from the voice of your conscience and free from the shadow of guilt. You are waiting because you want to be free to give all of yourself, not just a part in a panicking moment. Your own instincts tell you what a wonderful experience it could be, your first merger with another human being. And that same instinct keeps telling you not to waste it, not to hurry it, don't make it smog, or dirty. Wait...so that you can be free to give all of yourself, so that the ghost of guilt won't be hunting you!"

Or consider the story of two neighborhood girlfriends who shared a lot of their life together. They had grown up together through puberty and adolescence. These girls were smart in school, talented and popular. They had plans and worked hard at reaching goals at school and in their community. As close friends do, they shared a lot of personal things. They encouraged each other and looked out for each other at every turn. They even determined to keep themselves until the day they each found that special guy to marry. Now, both age 17 and about to graduate from high school, one of the girls had fallen deeply in love. As it is often the case, the girl thought she had found the right one. The young man in this girl's life was a very decent guy. He was a football player, and he was also a gentleman who did things to make the girl feel special. Unfortunately, the best friend sensed that the guy was coming between them. Her only concern was that perhaps they would get too serious about each other before the appropriate time. In a matter of time, that's exactly what happened. Within months the young girl came to her best friend shattered that she and her first love had broken up, and it seemed that it was indeed over for good. The real heartbreak was that she had given in to this guy and was no longer a virgin. As the weeks and days went by, the young girl began to mend and heal from her relationship that had turned sour. She talked to her friend and began to realize that perhaps she had even been used by a smooth talking Don Juan who only wanted the girl's body, instead of the special relationship that she wanted to last forever in her life. One thing is for sure, some people (whether in their conscious or subconscious mind), when it comes to relationships, are only playing games. They have no intentions of establishing a meaningful relationship. They are just looking to have fun or to see just where the relationship will go. Both trains of thought are disastrous because someone always ends up getting hurt.

Her way of reasoning and trying to make some sense of her error was to say to her friend, "At least I know what it's like to have slept with a guy. I have experienced something that you can only wonder about." Her friend's reply was, "Yes, you're right, but I have something that you can never have to give again … my chastity." The young girl went on to tell her friend, "And when you find the right one to spend your life with, keep in mind you will also bring who you thought was your first love into that relationship." And that can cause problems forever. That's why the Bible says, "Flee fornication. Every sin that a man doeth is without the body; but he that committeth fornication sinneth against his own body" (1 Corinthians 6:18). In other words, "keep yourself pure." I can't fully explain it and I'm sure I don't fully understand it, but know that you give yourself a real chance at Holy Matrimony when you can come into the relationship a complete person, unyielded to the temptations of sexual activities. You owe yourself that chance.

A few years ago a local AIDS Resource Council came up with the cutest yet thought provoking message about abstinence. Whereas the message was to guard against social diseases, it also serves to reserve one's morals as one travels through the rites of passage called adolescent courting. The message was entitled:

90 Ways to Make Love Without Doin' It

1) Tell the other person that you love them
2) Give or get a hug
3) Make the other person feel important and respected
4) Kiss
5) Have fun together
6) Tell the other person that you care
7) Hold hands
8) Go for a long bike ride
9) Make and give a special gift
10) Be there when a friend is needed
11) Spend time together
12) Go to a movie
13) Make a special tape of love songs
14) Talk openly about your feelings
15) Share dreams with each other
16) Snuggle up together
17) Sit together in the park
18) Take a walk together
19) Go out to eat
20) Have a picnic
21) Play a game of Frisbee
22) Give compliments
23) Relax in a whirlpool
24) Go swimming
25) Just be close
26) Go grocery shopping
27) Cook a meal together

28) Touch each other in a loving way
29) Do homework together
30) Plan and go on a road trip together
31) Throw a party together
32) Bake cookies
33) Go to the library
34) Browse in a museum
35) Just be there
36) Exercise together
37) Gaze at each other
38) Wash each other's car
39) Go fishing
40) Talk to each other
41) Do a work project together
42) Choose a special, favorite song
43) Hold one another close
44) Use eye contact to share a private thought
45) Write each other letters
46) Talk on the telephone
47) Trust one another
48) Meet each other's family
49) Go hiking together
50) Make sacrifices for each other
51) Send candy
52) Respect each other
53) Go for a moonlight walk
54) Hide a love note where the other will find it
55) Give each other sexy looks
56) Write a poem
57) Send flowers
58) Eat dinner by candlelight
59) Go to a concert
60) Watch the sunrise together
61) Take a drive together
62) Go sightseeing
63) Rent a video
64) Do things for each other without being asked

65) Propose marriage
66) Whisper something nice into the other's ear
67) Be best friends
68) Go out dancing
69) Play music together
70) Flirt with each other
71) Laugh at something funny together
72) Be faithful
73) Impress each other
74) Make a list of things you like about each other
75) Read a book and discuss it
76) Meet each other's friends
77) Cook each other's favorite food
78) Find out what makes the other happy
79) Make each other gifts
80) Be caring
81) Watch the sunset
82) Dedicate a song on the radio
83) Send a funny card
84) Share lifetime goals with each other
85) Play "footsies"
86) Share private jokes
87) Think about each other
88) Find out what makes the other sad
89) Share an ice cream
90) Have your picture taken together

Use your imagination with these ideas. Some of these you have to work at to do just one time. Some you can do over and over again. Some people may be able to snuggle and touch. Others may see touching as a very limited or off limits activity. You must determine how far you can go. Let these ideas trigger some other things for you to do without getting into trouble. It should also serve to heighten your expectation for when you are finally ready to settle down with your soul mate. I want you to also keep in mind that you're not alone. I've heard statements that almost seem like clichés: "Everybody's doing it" or "There are no more virgins." This simply is not true. You can be counted among a great (if not a large) number of people who understand that sex without the sanction of God's love is indeed just an animalistic act, primitive and selfish at best.

I know that someone might be saying, "But I have already made the mistake of giving myself over to sexual acts; it's too late for me." No, it's not too late for you. Remember I confessed that I, too, as a teenager, because of my lustful nature, self-centeredness and sheer ignorance, was sexually active before I was married. It was also at this time that I rededicated my life to Christ and asked Him to forgive me of my sins, which also included my sexual acting out. And although I have had some difficult days because of my sins, I know my sins were forgiven and I could start over with a clean slate. You must understand, if you are truly sorry for what you've done, Christ will be faithful to forgive and give you a fresh start. Periodically, we all need that fresh start, especially when getting serious with a partner.

No one should enter a relationship with past indiscretions (sin) weighing on their heart and mind. Yes, you can begin again as if you had never committed these acts. That's the goodness of God and the beginning of getting to know who you are. 1 John 1:9 says, "If we confess our sins, he is faithful and just to forgive us our sins, and to cleanse us from all unrighteousness." So if you have found someone and you truly believe that this person is the right one, then give all of your old habits, your sexual indiscretions, and all sin to God and ask forgiveness; then go on and live your life. If you believe God has forgiven you, don't let anyone put you down, and don't you put yourself down. Some teenagers don't have a clue as to what it really means to be in love and to make a commitment. Get on with your life, and don't make the same mistakes over and over again.

So it's only when you know yourself that you can truly know what you want in a partner. When you know yourself, then you know your likes and dislikes. Let's face a real fact: A cat lover might have problems being the partner of someone who's allergic to cats and generally hates animals as pets. Or even if some opposites attract, you must know what it is that's important to you so that you can communicate that to your partner.

Know yourself so that you can be yourself. Respect yourself and you will be able to express yourself. Know what you want to do, and as someone has said, "To thine own self be true." When you know who you are, then perhaps you have a better idea of the kind of person you want and need to share with in this adventure we call life.

Jan M. Summers is a poet who has been writing poetry and children's stories since 1987. Her poem, *"Do You Qualify?"* raises the right questions to people serious about getting married.

Do You Qualify?

Do you qualify to be the man I need you to be?
Will you be able to recognize the things you need to see?
Will you be able to understand that I'm a good woman and in
    my life I need a good man?
Do you qualify?
Do you qualify to fertilize my unproduced seeds?
Can you fulfill, as I can, all of our needs?
Can you put me in my place if you see I am slippin?
Can you talk to me, whole-heartedly, not constantly trippin?
Do you qualify?
Do you qualify to be called all mine?
Can you leave the other women and temptations behind?
Can you come to me with your problems and not wait until it's
    too late?
Can you stand up and admit if you made a mistake?
Do you qualify?
Do you qualify to be the honest ebony man I would want you to
    be?
Would you be able to look me in my eyes and admit your feel-
    ings to me?
Could you take me in your arms and make love to me all night
    long?
Can you be sensitive and still be strong?
Do you qualify?

Do you qualify to be my friend as well as my lover?
Can you put our love before any other?
Can you cherish me as if I were Diamonds & Gold?
Can you make me feel like I'm the last woman you'll ever hold?
Do you qualify?
Do you qualify to be called a good man?
If I have doubts, can you reassure me and understand?
Can your love intoxicate me as if I were High?
To be in my life, I need to know, DO YOU QUALIFY?

CHAPTER TWO

Understanding Just What Marriage Is

In my 23 years of ministry, I have been privileged to marry sixty couples. Unfortunately, a high percentage of those couples have not remained together. It bothers me when I see one of the partners at the grocery store or out in public and ask how they are doing, only to find out that their marriage has ended in divorce court. This has affected me in the worst way. I realize that as a minister, I am either a helper or a part of the demise of people I join together in marriage. In recent years I've begun to spend more time in counseling sessions with couples. I've come to realize that in many instances, people who were coming to me to get married didn't have a clue as to what it really meant to be united in Holy Matrimony. Most don't understand that marriage is holy and sacred. It is a very special walk through life with someone, that must be sanctioned by God if it is to have a chance at success. One partner might well be in love, while the other is in lust. Some people get married because it's a thing of convenience.

When I was in the military back in the early 1980's, I knew several couples who got married because in the military, married people are paid more money. There were some pretty decent people who took advantage of that for the sake of money. These couples might have been friends, but they were not in love with each other. In one instance, an unwanted child was born to a couple. One couple got a divorce when their tour of duty was up because that was what they agreed to do.

Some people get married to the first person who shows interest in them, because they feel that it's some terrible shame to be single past the age of 21. Other couples marry knowing that they are not in love, but they want to impress their friends.

I never shall forget the day I married a couple and the bride was literally mad at the groom. They were not happy, they were not at peace, they were mad. I thought to myself, "What in the world am I doing in the middle of this fiasco?"

I must also confess that on one occasion I married a couple and the groom reeked with liquor. He wasn't staggering, but he was drunk. I was so embarrassed for the bride. I honestly did not know what to do. I didn't realize he was intoxicated until he blew his liquor breath in my face. I wasn't a mature preacher back then. I did a lot of couples a grave injustice by marrying them. The bottom line: too many people get married for all the wrong reasons. That is to say too many couples don't understand the meaning of marriage. What, then, is marriage? What is this institution we call Holy Matrimony?

If it is my belief that marriage is supposed to be forever, then you've got to understand that to me marriage is the second most important decision you'll ever make. (Your decision to live for Christ is the most important.)

Now the only real definition of marriage must come from the Bible because God instituted this way of life between man and woman. As a matter of fact, the scriptures clearly point out that the woman came out of the man's side (she was formed from one of his ribs) with the distinct purpose of being his help meet. Look at the scripture and observe the simplicity of why, what, and how God introduced woman to man. "And the LORD God said, It is not good that the man should be alone; I will make him an help meet for him" (Genesis 2:18). Genesis 2:21-25 states, "And the LORD God caused a deep sleep to fall upon Adam, and he slept: and he took one of his ribs, and closed up the flesh instead thereof; And the rib, which the LORD God had taken from man, made he a woman, and brought her unto the man. And Adam said, This is now bone of my bones, and flesh of my flesh: she shall be called Woman, because she was taken out of Man. Therefore shall a man leave his father and his mother, and shall cleave unto his wife: and they shall be one flesh. And they were both naked, the man and his wife, and were not ashamed."

Now I am writing from my heart, based on my own experiences.

I am sharing with people who believe they are in love, that if you can grasp what the marriage institution is all about, you stand a good chance of making a good life with that someone who is special to you. The marriage institution is really basic and simple for those individuals who are willing to humble themselves to sound, sensible advice, and are willing to be patient with each other. That said, let me get back to making my point: marriage was and continues to be God's way of giving the man he created a companion. God determined that man needed something else, and this turned out to be someone who could help him in having dominion over the Earth and things of the Earth. "Therefore shall a man leave his father and his mother, and shall cleave unto his wife: and they shall be one flesh." That verse is so important that it is repeated again in the New Testament by our Lord and Savior, Jesus Christ. Plus, he adds a very staunch declarative statement about the eternalism of marriage. "For this cause shall a man leave father and mother, and shall cleave to his wife: and they twain shall be one flesh? Wherefore they are no more twain, but one flesh. What therefore God hath joined together, let not man put asunder" (Matthew 19:5, 6).

The Apostle Paul suggests in his writings that in heaven no one marries or is given in marriage; but the marriage vows say until death do you part. This is why I declare that marriage is a very serious matter, because marriage is suppose to be forever, which is to say until one is taken in death.

I've used the following quote from *The Star Book of Ministers*, by Edward T. Hiscox, to begin most of the wedding ceremonies that I've performed: "Divine Revelation has declared marriage to be honorable in all. It is an institution of God, ordained in the time of man's innocence, before he had sinned against his Maker, and been yet banished from Paradise. It was given in wisdom and in kindness, to repress irregular affection, to support social order, and to provide that, through well-ordered families, truth and holiness might be transmitted from one age to another. Earlier, therefore, than all laws of merely human origin, it lies at the basis of all human legislation and civil government, and the peace and well-being of the nation and land."

I've come to realize that marriage is not just for the two people who are making a commitment; its purpose serves the whole of society. Marriage is the prerequisite to the family. I don't think I'm original in this train of thought, but I know this is true. The family unit shapes the churches and neighborhoods; churches and neighborhoods shape communities. The communities determine the kind of city you live in. Then, the cities shape the states, and the states shape our nation. Finally, it is the nations that shape the kind of world we live in. But it all starts with the family unit. If God orders the families, that is to say if a husband and wife are God-fearing and committed to godly principles, then the nation will be highly favored of God. This ensures times of peace and prosperity (at the least within the marriage). On the other side of the coin, show me a country where divorce rates are high and families are dysfunctional, then I will show you a nation headed for doom.

It is through marriage that men and women consummate their love, start families by having children, and reinforce their love for each other through intimate contact. These very passionate, sensual, and personal acts are one way God gives our lives order and meaning. That is to say that only when two people are joined in the bonds of holy matrimony is their intimacy truly special. Marriage is holy and sacred. It is a very special walk through life that must be sanctioned by God if it is to have a chance at success.

A family comes to mind that exemplifies for me the power of family impacting the community around it. As I stated earlier, I attended the Springfield Baptist Church every Sunday. The Olivers were members of Springfield. The father of the family was Evins Oliver. "Dee" Oliver, as he was affectionately called, worked at the local G.E. plant. He was the Chairman of the Deacon's Board, and the Sunday School Superintendent. I know the Ten Commandments right now because every Sunday morning, as part of his Sunday School opening, he would read those commandments. Moses might have written them, but I dare say nobody recited the Ten Commandments more than Deacon Oliver. His wife, Elizabeth, taught the primary class in Sunday School, and she sang in the choir. We called her Sister Oliver. Now to my knowledge Sister Oliver was a housewife, and that's all. I mean she didn't iron, wash anybody's clothes, or do domestic work other than for her family. I highlight this because there is something to be said about a woman who is privileged to stay at home and be a housewife and mother. For one thing, she was the comforter of the home. Do you know any women who are housewives? Observe the relaxed atmosphere of a home where the mother gets to stay at home. In most homes, a housewife keeps things calm and in order.

The Oliver's had five children: Fred (the oldest), Mable, Shirley, Marvin, and Tony (the baby). Shirley is perhaps three or four years older than I am, while Marvin was a couple of years younger. Coming from a broken home and at times a dysfunctional family, I could always look to the Olivers and be encouraged. I wasn't the only one who admired them, and perhaps I was even jealous of them because I was rather immature.

They were indeed a model family. There were other families who were truly good examples, but the Olivers just stood out. They were leaders. I remember Fred as the great basketball player and captain of the team at dear old Main High School. Main High was the local high school for blacks before integration. Mable was a charmette, something similar to a social climber, and a sweetheart on campus. She was pretty and the epitome of elegance and grace. Mable was a quiet leader. She played the piano in church. She led not by what she said, but by what she did not say. Even to this day, when Mable comes into a room, she brings a certain elegance and dignity that only Christian ladies have. Then there was Shirley, who was Miss Congeniality at school. She was smart, pretty, a cheerleader, and she could play the piano and sing. Most of all it was obvious that she loved every minute of whatever she was doing.

Then there was Marvin, who was like a little brother to me. I admired him so because he seemed to genuinely like me just for who I was–a regular guy. Tony is the one that I knew the least about, but he was an Oliver and fun to be around. I remember Tony primarily as a quiet and good guy who grew up to be bigger than all of us and play a mean game of football. You can imagine this family operating in the church, the school, and the neighborhood–they were special. I'm sure they had problems, but you never heard it. There was only one man working in this family of seven. Fred and Marvin might have helped their dad clean offices when they were old enough, but Dee Oliver basically provided for his family. Yet, they managed to do as well as, if not better than, anyone else in the neighborhood. They always seemed to stand out because that parental guidance and support was very much in place. As I was growing up, I could look to this family and say "Wow, this is how I want my family to be." No doubt about it, I wanted to be just like Dee Oliver–a godly man and a family man. I wanted my wife to be just like Sister Oliver–a church worker, housewife, and devoted mother. I knew in the very depths of my soul that if I could be half as dedicated as Dee Oliver, I could have a chance at being a church man and a family man. I don't know if Mr. and Mrs. Oliver ever attended college, but their children did. That family has produced teachers, principals, nurses, and semi-professional singers; but, most importantly, all their families are intact. And, another generation of Oliver offsprings are making their way through this adventure we call life. The most important thing is they all love the Lord, they are family and they look to each other for support, even to this day. In the spring of 1999, Dee Oliver went home to glory to be with the Lord. He and his sweet wife were married for more than 56 years. The Oliver Story is what marriage and family is all about.

So although marriage is a very personal bond between the man and the woman, a marriage ordained of God also serves as a very public example of how people ought to live in society. A good marriage, a successful marriage, inspires others to want to have the same thing. What many fail to understand is that marriage is work. There is a lot of trial and error. There are trials and tribulations, and it takes time. However, if two people are willing to work at it, marriage can work. It's not a challenge; it's the challenge of your life. Even the vows declare it: For richer or poorer for better or for worse, in sickness and in health, until death do you part. It's a divine partnership, or a partnership ordained by God; and if you live as He has ordered, it becomes a sweet, blissful relationship unique unto the partners involved. The meaning of life and lifestyles are clearly defined again and again in marriages. This is why I can declare that "marriage is supposed to be forever."

I don't know if I thought of this myself or if someone shared this with me, but I do have an explanation of marriage that I have shared with all couples that I have been privileged to counsel over the years. It's what I call "From the Roller Coaster to the Plane Ride Marriage." Be aware that initially a marriage is like a roller coaster ride. That is to say that the relationship is full of ups and downs. It may go for days, maybe even months where everything is going up, up, and up. Neither mate can do anything wrong. You're inseparable. It is just a good time. You can't get enough of each other, and you value each other's every train of thought. But at some point there will be a disagreement, a spat, a falling out and a falling away. It could be one thing or a series of things that are like a long ride down from the top of the roller coaster. And you'll know when this roller coaster ride has hit rock bottom. Now you don't stay at the bottom. You don't stay mad–you forgive, you make up, and you work things out. And you begin your ascension up the roller coaster again until it peaks at the top. Before you know it, you're laughing and happy. But then here comes the descent to the bottom again. Generally, it can be over the smallest of things: He left the lid up on the toilet. She burned the rice. He thinks out loud, "How do you burn rice?" The ride is at the bottom again. Hopefully the ride gradually grows to where there are more days of climbing and peaking at the top than descending to and stalling at the bottom of the roller coaster. Some people can sustain the good ride for long periods of time, yet when they fall, it becomes a horrible experience. Then for some couples, it seems that every single day is an up and down, up and down roller coaster ride. On this roller coaster ride one of two things is established: (1) Mates learn to live on a roller coaster ride relationship; or (2) One spouse decides at some point that it's time to get off the ride. Needless to say, neither one of these responses is what you want in a marriage that you want to last forever.

This is where the plane ride comes into play. Yes, rather than ride a roller coaster, see your marriage as a plane ride, which clearly means that you are working toward a relationship that is forever upward and onward until you choose together to land and settle issues. It is said that a plane is most vulnerable at take-off, which says to me that marriages are most vulnerable in the early stages–not during the honeymoon period, but those first few years when you are settling down and really getting to know the person you have chosen to live your life with. A plane take-off is relatively slow at first–only when all systems are go does the plane move to a speed that allows it to go airborne. Once in the air, the pilot and co-pilot are constantly checking the gauges on the plane to make sure all is running according to the flight plans. Every now and then, the plane will naturally run into some bad weather–rough winds that will cause some uncomfortable moments–but the pilot and the co-pilot work together to guide the plane through the turbulence. In many instance, they fly higher to get out of the storm. Have you ever heard of planes dropping in altitude to get out of a storm? Maybe they do, but my experience on planes is that they go higher. In marriages, when you set your sights on things above the storms, you are generally able to move away from the turbulence. My point is...learn to make your marriage a plane ride instead of a roller coaster ride. Don't live on that emotional roller coaster where you are easily upset about trivial things. Recognize that in relationships, you will have disagreements. Disagree over things, but always agree to be friends and love each other. Attack the problems, situations, and circumstances that arise, but never attack each other. Get on the plane and determine that you are going to move upward and onward always. When there is rough turbulence, work together to get through the storms. See your marriage as a plane ride, headed for your planned destinations.

    Let me close this chapter by telling you a story of a unique couple. It is a beautiful story that demonstrates to some degree just what marriage is all about. Ted and Alice had been going together for almost two years now. Alice was finishing college and was going to be a teacher. Ted had not gone to college but was a hard worker. He had his own small jewelry business, and he was doing well. So one summer night in the month of June, Ted asked Alice to marry him. She certainly told him yes and was excited about their engagement. She began immediately to make plans. Her family joined in the excitement and planning for a December wedding.

Ted likewise had saved enough money to make a down payment on the purchase of a small but new home for them to move into when they were married. Everything was falling into place, and most of all, they genuinely loved one another. They were both Christians and were involved in the church. Alice worked with children's church, and Ted sang in the Young Adult choir. They worked together in the youth department. Just a typical yet special couple looking forward with great anticipation to a married life together. However, their plans were altered one Friday night after a high school football game in early September. Ted had played football, and kept up with and supported his high school alma mater. He was headed over to Alice's house and had planned to take her out for a late dinner. As it often happens, a drunk driver swilled into an oncoming lane and crashed head-on into Ted, paralyzing him from the waist down. You can imagine the devastation. This young couple had so much to look forward to; a relationship with so much promise. All this was put on hold because of a drunk driver. It was most difficult the first month. Ted had to fight for his life. Then they all came to realize that Ted would survive, but would probably never walk or have use of his body below the waist. You can imagine that this hit Ted pretty hard. Alice was the great support that only a young girl in love could be. She was most mature for her age. It was her first year teaching and she had the good spirit and grace of God to handle teaching and being there for her boyfriend and not miss a cue. It was special.

It had been two months since the accident, and the wedding was three months away. Everything had been put on hold because of Ted's condition. He was now heavily involved in rehabilitation, trying to learn how to survive without the use of his lower extremities. Ted was bitter some days, but by now he had accepted his cross. He wanted to get on with his life, whatever he had left of it, and whatever it might hold. It was at this point in his life, that he shared with Alice what he had been thinking about from the moment he learned he could not walk or use his lower body. Because of his present condition (not being able to engage in sexual activities, give Alice any children, or even share basic things like a walk through the park with her), Ted desired to release her from their engagement so that she could be free to have the "normal" life they had planned. Further, he wanted to get on with the rehabilitation of his life. He wanted to learn to drive. He wanted to be as independent as possible. He knew that marriage was out of the question, in December or any other time. Ted had the courage to say all of these things to the girl of his dreams, the woman he only months ago had asked to be his wife. When Alice realized what Ted was doing, she couldn't help but cry. And as they embraced and Ted talked about being good friends, Alice hushed his voice with a kiss. Then she took him and held him in her bosom and whispered to him, "As long as I have breath and strength to hold you, I will. If you will only give us a chance, I know that our love will find a way to an abundance of life, and that with happiness." Needless to say, Ted and Alice were married as planned on Christmas Day. Even until this day (some fifteen years later), they are indeed together with an abundance of life and happiness.

Ted and Alice understand what it means to be committed, loyal, dedicated, and in love with each other. That love is indeed a gift from God. People that use this gift must hope for all things, believe in all things, bear all things, and endure all things. Love always finds a way to keep its commitment. Love finds a way to put the other partner first. Love finds a way to be unselfish, caring, and giving. Love is a gift from God, when shared unconditionally with that special person. And if that partner dares to reciprocate and share love also, the couple grasps what it means to walk through life together. When there is a place and space in the heart; when what you feel for your beloved is unconditional; when you are willing to spend forever with that person, then that, my friend, is what marriage is all about.

CHAPTER THREE

Keep the Lines of Communication Open

I strongly believe that communication is key to the success of any endeavor. A person who knows how to express his/her ideas and points of view is going somewhere. If you are applying for a job or if you are working on a job, your prosperity or demise is in your ability to express yourself appropriately. If you want to buy a particular car or take a trip somewhere, or just go to a restaurant for lunch, you must be able to communicate what your thoughts are. I know now why the 3 R's (Reading, Writing, and Arithmetic) are essential to matriculate through school: these are the principals upon which communicating is built. Certainly, good communication skills are essential when it comes to having a harmonious relationship with a spouse.

I'm sure no one will argue with me when I tell you that in a relationship, the worst thing you and your spouse could do is to stop talking to each other. I never shall forget the first two years of my marriage–I call them the roller coaster years. When there were rough times, I would simply stop talking and pout. That's right, a grown man walking around with his lips protruding and a chip on his shoulder. Maybe we couldn't agree on what we were going to do for the holidays. Or perhaps she wore my favorite dress shirt without my permission. We would argue about surface things; not serious issues at all.

I must confess, early in my marriage I pouted and blamed my wife to cover my problems and insecurities. Anyway, something would happen that would send me into this mode where I would say to myself, "I don't have to take this from her. I'll show her, I'll just stop speaking for a while." And that's exactly what I'd do. I'd get up in the morning with the silent treatment. She naturally would follow my lead and also stop talking to me. I assume her thinking was, "If he doesn't speak to me, then I'm not speaking to him." We would prepare for work, eat breakfast and not one word was said between us. Isn't that terrible? But I promise you, it happens. And for my wife and me, it would go on for days. If I spoke, it would only be for things of necessity. For example, if her mother called, when she got home I would say, "Your mother called," and that would be it. Maybe later I would ask where something was or if she planned to cook that night? The bottom line would be to say no more than necessary. This would go on for as long as one, two, maybe three days at the most.

Then it would happen. In simple terms, my hormones would kick in. To say it another way, my Eros love for my wife would beckon for intimacy with her. To break it on down, I would get the urge to merge. Now I suppose for lesser guys this would be their opportunity to cut out on their wives. Thank God I never saw that as an option. I would get mad and get quiet as a way of trying to get even, but cheating on my wife has never been an option for me. So after a few days I would swallow my pride. She's never admitted it, but I think the feeling was mutual. She always seemed receptive to my getting back in touch with her. It might happen one evening when we got off from work and I would simply greet her with a kiss and apologize. Maybe we would be watching TV and I would strike up a conversation and she would respond appropriately. When I would get lonesome for her, I would use any thing, any situation to open up the lines of communication. But the truth is, we should have never allowed ourselves to get to the point that we were not talking.

Have you ever thought that when you and your partner are not talking that there is another voice speaking to each of you? And that voice does not have the best interest of your relationship at heart. I heard an old preacher say that there is a misconception about how many partners are in a relationship. He said that most folks think there is only the husband and wife in a marriage; but there is a third person in every relationship. And the third person is really a spirit. The third person is a personality; a good or bad spirit that each partner brings into a relationship. I did not readily accept what that old preacher was saying for most of my marriage, but as I got older I realized that he was right on target. There is at least a third person or third influence in a marriage, and the influence can be overwhelming when partners are not talking.

If you are Christian in your thinking, you know exactly what the old preacher is saying. He's saying that each one of us brings Christ (the Holy Spirit, a positive spirit) or Satan (the bad or negative spirit) into our relationship. This is why your selection of a partner is so important.

When my wife and I celebrated our 25th Wedding Anniversary this year, one of our friends gave us a beautiful picture frame with the following poem:

MARRIAGE TAKES THREE

Marriage takes three to be complete;
It's not enough for two to meet. They must be
United in love by love's Creator, God above.
Then their love will be firm and strong;
Able to last when things go wrong,
Because they've felt God's love and know
He's always there; He'll never go.
And they have both loved Him in kind
With all the heart and soul and mind;
And in that love they've found the way
To love each other everyday,
A marriage that follows God's plan
Takes more than a woman and man.
It needs a oneness that can be
Only from Christ - Marriage Takes Three.

Beth Stuckwisch © Dicksons

Now if the man and woman are both Christian in nature, the potential to keep the lines of communication open at all times is great. Even if trouble arises, the Christ nature should find a way to talk through the problems. Now if one partner is Christian and the other is not, there is still hope because God promises to sanctify (cleanse) that relationship. It's like the old cowboy movies where the white hat identified the good cowboy. He always won out in the end and rode off into the sunset with another victory. The Bible infers that if one partner will hold up the Christian precepts, that ultimately he or she will win over the partner who does not have those same values. 1 Corinthians 7:12-17 says, "But to the rest speak I, not the Lord: If any brother hath a wife that believeth not, and she is pleased to dwell with him, let him not put her away. And the woman which hath an husband that believeth not, and if he be pleased to dwell with her, let her not leave him. For the unbelieving husband is sanctified by the wife, and the unbelieving wife is sanctified by the husband: else were your children unclean; but now are they holy. But if the unbelieving depart, let him depart. A brother or a sister is not under bondage in such cases: but God hath called us to peace. For what knowest thou, O wife, whether thou shalt save thy husband? or how knowest thou, O man, whether thou shalt save thy wife? But as God hath distributed to every man, as the Lord hath called every one, so let him walk. And so ordain I in all churches."

There is much discussion as to what that scripture really means. I am confident that its simplest meaning is that God will bless the relationship if one partner is faithful in living Christlike before his partner. Just be patient and keep the lines of communication open.

But say you have a situation where neither one of the partners are walking with God, then you have partners who stop talking and start pouting day in and day out. That was my case. My wife and I simply were not walking close enough to God to keep the lines of communication open. I stopped talking and she would follow my lead. (There's something to be said about that, and we'll address that in another chapter.) And when partners are not talking, that voice within begins talking to each partner.

This voice tends to keep up the silence between the two. This voice says simple things to you like, "Don't talk to her, you'll show her who's boss." This voice brings up things that happened yesterday or last week that you had said you were not going to deal with. This voice brings old things up from your past and tells you this is the time to deal with it. This voice becomes a voice of prophecy because it also starts to tell you what's going to happen in the future: "When she comes home today, you know she's not cooking dinner." So from 2:00 P.M. until you get home at 5:30 P.M., you are stewing over the fact that a voice has told you she is not going to cook. The truth is, you don't know whether she is going to cook or not, but the voice has planted the seed. Sometimes this voice will even tell you lies, and you'll believe them. For example, the phone might ring and because you haven't talked to her in two days, the voice tells you, "She must be talking to her boyfriend." If she's later than usual getting home from work and you haven't talked to her for a day or two, the voice declares, "She must have a love interest on her job." The voice desires and will literally drive you to fits of rage and jealousy simply by telling you, over and over again, the worst case scenario about your partner.

That particular voice is the voice of Satan, and when you stop talking to your partner, Satan starts talking to you. Always remember that Satan enters our being through the mind. If we do not have the mind of Christ, then we are in trouble, not only in marriage but in every facet of life. That's right, Satan always places thoughts in your mind that cause you to doubt what you already know is true.

Remember how he deceived Eve in Genesis 3. Satan always attacks us through the mind. I suppose this is why the Bible is full of scripture that calls for us to be like-minded, and of the same mind. There's a constant call for the renewing of your mind. And the scripture says that the mind of Christ keeps our minds renewed. "Let this mind be in you, which was also in Christ Jesus" (Philippians 2:5). I promise you if you have, your thinking is always of reconciliation–and that as soon as possible. When you think as Christ would think (which is to say as the Bible teaches), you are willing to submit–humbly, lowly, sweetly, and sincerely–seeking ways to be restored to your partner. It's no longer about trying to establish yourself as boss. You are not trying to win a battle, you just want to be loving and at peace with your spouse. And with the mind of Christ you soon learn how to keep the lines of communication open.

Now there are some practical things that the mind of Christ will help you to do. Since we are dealing with things of the mind, the first thing I want to suggest to you is to THINK before you speak. I can not begin to tell you how many times I have opened my mouth and said something that was fruitless and/or harmful. For example, never give your spouse money to go buy a dress or suit of their choice and then, upon their return, tell them you don't like what they purchased. Maybe you don't really mean anything by what you say, and are just giving your honest opinion, but remember, once those words leave your mouth, you can't take them back. Not liking a spouses selection after giving them a choice can be interpreted in so many ways. You might leave your spouse thinking you don't have confidence in their opinion of things, or that they have poor taste in clothes. This can lead to spouses having unhealthy attitudes about their choices in other matters or about themselves, all because you gave them the freedom of choice and then took it back with an insensitive statement. Let me give you another example. Never compare your wife's cooking to your mother's, even if you're joking or just having fun. The bottom line is that's not fair. Look at all the years of experience your mother has cooking. Your mother may love to cook. Your wife may not like cooking at all and sees cooking as a necessary chore to keep you happy. THINK before you speak because words do hurt. Listen to how the Bible describes the power of the tongue: "Even so the tongue is a little member, and boasteth great things. Behold, how great a matter a little fire kindleth! And the tongue is a fire, a world of iniquity: so is the tongue among our members, that it defileth the whole body, and setteth on fire the course of nature; and it is set on fire of hell. For every kind of beasts, and of birds, and of serpents, and of things in the sea, is tamed, and hath been tamed of mankind: But the tongue can no man tame; it is an unruly evil, full of deadly poison" (James 3:5-8).

THINK before you speak because words do hurt.

When I was growing up, the one theme of my personality expressed by all my teachers was that I had the "gift of gab." I literally talked all the time. I'm grateful for that today because as a preacher, I am talking for the right reasons and about the right things. However, I can remember long before I was a preacher how I had command of communicating my ideas to people. As I stated earlier, it was always important to me to be funny. I wasn't the class clown, but you could always count on me for a good laugh. Sometimes this would be at the expense of others. I developed a habit of being sarcastic about everything. Now, over the years, I've learned that sarcasm is just a funny way of putting people down. Hopefully, my days of putting people down are behind me, but how many times do I hear it in casual conversation. Sarcasm can destroy a marriage. Don't ever use sarcasm in conversation with your spouse unless you are sure the partner is in a good mood and ready to deal with it. Nobody wants to be at the other end of the joke, no matter how harmless it is. Too many times sarcasm is simply telling someone in a funny way what you don't have the courage to tell them otherwise. Nobody wants to be the butt end of another person's jokes; not one time, not ever. Certainly this does not build or strengthen your relationship. I'm not saying that you can't joke with each other. There is plenty of room to enjoy jokes, kidding, and humor in relationships; but don't use these things to the point that they become put downs and expressions of criticism to the ones you love and hold in high esteem.

Another point that comes to mind is…when you and your partner are having conversations, particularly about sensitive areas like finances, friends, or personal differences of opinion, remember this: "It's not what you say, it's how you say it."

You might not think so at first but I promise you, the ones we love the most are oftentimes the ones we hurt the most, not because of what we say, but how we say it. I know that is true in my life. My darling wife has endured the whip of my quick-witted tongue lashing for 25 years. I've been guilty of letting my emotions override my rational thinking. Therefore, instead of having clear, sensible, tempered conversations, I would turn them into loud, unproductive shouting outbursts. And when the dust settled, the issues were not worth the trouble.

Constant bickering, arguing, and fussing never resolve anything because no one is listening, everyone is shouting out their point of view. However, there is some resolve for this verbal abuse. The scripture says, "A soft answer turneth away wrath: but grievous words stir up anger" (Proverbs 15:1). I don't remember where I first heard this statement, but it is so true: "It takes two to argue." Any time you want to be the one who stops the verbal abusing in your relationship, just stop arguing and begin to use soft tones. I promise you, that works. I am speaking from experience. For years I would rant and rave about stupid stuff. I would fuss if Judy spent more money at the grocery store than I thought she should have. I would get upset if I checked her car and found the oil was a quart low. I've fussed if she and our small kids weren't ready for church when I was. I don't know where she got it from, and I can't remember when it first started, but there came a time when Judy just would not get caught up in my emotions with regard to things that apparently nobody could do anything about. She learned how to keep her cool when I was having fits. And in a very short period of time, I stopped my tirades because I realized quickly how foolish I looked, sounded, and indeed was acting. THINK before you speak, and when you do speak, relax and watch how you present your point of view. You never have to get mad or belittle others when things don't work out the way you think they should. Learn how to express yourself without getting emotionally out of control in the process.

Finally, you keep the lines of communication open when you learn not to bear grudges. Some things we simply chalk up to experience, and let them go. There is a verse of scripture that comes to mind that serves as a rule to help people who tend to want to bear grudges and let things go on and on: "Be ye angry, and sin not: let not the sun go down upon your wrath (Ephesians 4:26). I really believe that the times will come in relationships that you will get upset–angry. Apparently there is a way to get angry without sinning. The inference is don't stew over things too long. Don't let your anger linger. Recognize what's happening to you, then begin the process of relaxing. I guess this is where counting to ten or taking deep breaths makes sense. Do what you need to do to deflate your anger. Next, try to define the issue and seek to resolve it, at least to the point where you and your spouse are communicating sensibly and with love.

Judy and I have an understanding that we never allow anything or anyone outside our home to disturb the peace within our home. No matter what the crisis or frustration, we choose not to go to bed mad or angry. If you are big enough not to bear grudges, then you can keep the lines of communication open.

CHAPTER FOUR

Duties of the Husband & Wife

Our God is a God of order. It is my belief that in the realm of God, few things are by chance; most things are tailor-made, ordained by an all-seeing, all-knowing, and all-powerful God. God knows what's best for us. This is why it is important that as you deal with the things of God (like courtship and marriage), it becomes imperative that you have a relationship with God through Jesus Christ as your personal Savior. Why? Because He gives order in the relationship and through Him I've found that things make sense.

Romans 8:29, 30 states, "For whom he did foreknow, he also did predestinate to be conformed to the image of his Son, that he might be the firstborn among many brethren. Moreover, whom he did predestinate, them he also called: and whom he called, them he also justified: and whom he justified, them he also glorified." Ephesians 1:11 further states, "In whom also we have obtained an inheritance, being predestinated according to the purpose of him who worketh all things after the counsel of his own will." Psalm 37:23 says, "The steps of a good man are ordered by the LORD: and he delighteth in his way."

You believe me when I tell you our God is a God of order. Spring always follows winter, summer always follows spring. Fall always follows summer, and winter always follows fall because God is a God of order. The earth rotates on it's axis every 24 hours, making one day and one night. This has been happening since God first said "let there be…" Why? God is a God of order.

Well then, if order is imperative in the realm of God, how did he order the relationship of man and woman? What, then, is the order of husband and wife? You will recall Genesis 2:21 talks about man leaving his mother and father to cleave unto himself a wife, and the twain shall be one flesh. This is a result of the first woman, Eve, being made by God from one of Adam's ribs. Let's back up to Genesis 2:18 and see what the order is: "And the LORD God said, It is not good that the man should be alone; I will make him a help meet for him." Matthew Henry's Commentary explains this verse: "Power over the creatures was given to man, and as a proof of this he named them all. It also shows his insight into the works of God. But though he was lord of the creatures, yet nothing in this world was a help meet for man. From God are all our helpers. If we rest in God, he will work all for good. God caused deep sleep to fall on Adam; while he knows no sin, God will take care that he shall feel no pain. God, as her Father, brought the woman to the man, as his second self and as a help meet for him. That wife, who is of God's making by special grace, and of God's bringing by special providence, is likely to prove a help meet for a man."

The woman's role (especially in matters of the home, church and spirituality) is to be the helpmate to her man. This was God's first and original intent for woman. I think we should be cautious not to tamper with the original intent of God. "Forever, O LORD, thy word is settled in heaven" (Psalm 119:89).

That is not to say that a woman is not an equal human being. I have heard it said that the only real difference between man and woman is a "womb." That is to say that the woman has the womb in order that human being's offspring can be birthed into the world. Generally speaking, women are capable of doing anything men do (positions of physical strength being the exception). This is not about pointing out any gender inferiority. This is about performing duties and understanding the roles husbands and wives are called upon to play. It's about the order of things. Marriage is about understanding the roles we are called upon to play from the very beginning. It's about how God blesses when we stay in His order and how we suffer when we get out of His order.

If you were to read Genesis the third chapter, you would see that mankind lost fellowship with God when they did not follow the order of things. Eve was guilty of listening to a voice that was not her husband's. Adam was guilty of allowing his wife to persuade him to do something that he knew was a settled issue between he and God: "But of the fruit of the tree which is in the midst of the garden, God hath said, Ye shall not eat of it, neither shall ye touch it, lest ye die" (Genesis 2:17).

Notice what punishment is given to Adam and Eve for getting out of His divine order and His divine will after they ate from the tree of the knowledge of Good and Evil: "Unto the woman he said, I will greatly multiply thy sorrow and thy conception; in sorrow thou shalt bring forth children; and thy desire shall be to thy husband, and he shall rule over thee. And unto Adam he said, Because thou hast hearkened unto the voice of thy wife, and hast eaten of the tree, of which I commanded thee, saying, Thou shalt not eat of it: cursed is the ground for thy sake; in sorrow shalt thou eat of it all the days of thy life" (Genesis 3:16, 17).

So since the beginning of time, God has ordained an order as to how He wants the relationship between a husband and his wife to be. And when Adam and Eve strayed from that order, mankind paid the consequences, even to this day.

So what does God require of the husband and wife in order that their relationship might be as He intended it to be? Well, let's look at some New Testament scripture that continues to define the duties of husband and wife. "For the husband is the head of the wife, even as Christ is the head of the church: and he is the savior of the body. Therefore as the church is subject unto Christ, so let the wives be to their own husbands in every thing" (Ephesians 5:23, 24).

Now the first thing that I want to suggest is that this scripture is misinterpreted by most people and leaves a bad taste in the mouths of wives because they aren't really grasping what this means. For the husband is the head of the wife, even as Christ is the head of the church.

Husbands, being the head of the wife as Christ is the Head of the Church is no easy chord. Being called upon to do something as Christ does should bring about profound humility. That Christ would ask of me to love my wife as He loves the church should serve as an instant attitude adjustment. Men, we are going to love our wives as Christ loves the church. However difficult the task may seem, it is imperative that man readily accepts his role. Now what was Christ's role as the head of the Church? Well, you know the church is often referred to as the bride of Christ, and He demonstrates divine love for the church. It is an unconditional love. It's a love that says, "I love you not just because of what you do, but in spite of things you fail to do, I love you." Christ established the church, nurtures the church, heals the church, prays for the church, provides for and protects the church; and in the end he died for the church that the church through him and by him might be saved (Ephesians 5:26, 27).

Notice what is said in Ephesians 5:28: "So ought men to love their wives as their own bodies. He that loveth his wife loveth himself." Have you ever thought that your wife is an extension of you? In your proper frame of mind you would never curse yourself, abuse yourself, or ignore basic things about yourself that make your life complete. Neither would you deny yourself basic necessities to make your daily living a pleasant and positive experience. Therefore, you would never treat your wife that way either because she is the extension of you. In the book *Married for Life*, by Mike and Marilyn Phillipps, it states, "You are one flesh in two bodies."[1]

I have not always understood this, but it's clear to me now. As a husband, it is my responsibility, obligation, and duty to provide for my wife the best possible lifestyle I can. I should joyfully nurture her, bring healing for her emotional wounds, provide spiritual guidance for her, and protect and shelter her from any and every thing that would hinder her from being the best person she can be. Then I understand that I must encourage and promote those things that will help her to be the best person she can be. Ultimately, I must give my life that she might live that abundant life that Jesus promised.

Now ladies, how can I explain to you that there is nothing belittling about submitting to and obeying a God-fearing man? Let the scriptures be your guide: "Submitting yourselves one to another in the fear of God. Wives, submit yourselves unto your own husbands, as unto the Lord" (Ephesians 5:21, 22). The

---

[1] Mike and Marilyn Phillips, *Married for Life* (Littleton, Colorado: Eden Publishing, 1996).

end to which all things ought to be referred, to serve one another for God's sake.

What this clearly says to me is that after the husband and wife have counseled with each other, or even debated some issues, the husband is the God-appointed representative or spokesperson in the relationship. This doesn't mean that the wife is not capable of being the spokesperson. Just know that in the final analysis, God holds the husband responsible for his family; therefore, when it comes to the family, the man is held accountable first, woman second.

Wives, you should have no problems with the word "submit" if your husband has submitted to God and the things of God. A God-fearing man is going to love his wife unconditionally. How? He gets his example from Christ. Being the head of the wife should not be interpreted as "bossing her around." He's not to ignore her feelings and make every decision about every matter. I am the head of my wife; and as a godly man, and because of my love and respect for her opinions, I always share and consult with her on everything concerning our family. I cannot begin to count the times that my wife's suggestions went against my personal train of thought. Yet decisions we've made together were generally the right ones.

Submitting to your husband is accepting his covering, his shelter, and his protection. As Christ does, a man must literally give up his life that his wife and family might be sheltered and protected both spiritually and physically.

Wives, your duties are to love, cherish, honor, and obey him. And obeying and being submissive to a God-fearing man should not be a problem at all. Why? Because your husband is always looking out for your best interests, you know this and he knows this. Let me ask you something ladies: Do you obey the word of God? Do you love God and obey the Father in heaven? Then you should have no problem obeying the husband that God has given you. Help your man to be the spiritual leader of your house. How? Encourage him and be patient with him. Exchange ideas, and when you make decisions together, help him to follow through on the plan. But most of all, support him. In other words, give him your loyalty, give him your trust, give him praises and he will (or should) respond appropriately. The relationship becomes a beautiful walk.

Some of the most valuable scriptures in the Bible, to a woman, are those that talk about a virtuous woman: "Who can find a virtuous woman? For her price is far above rubies. The heart of her husband doth safely trust in her, so that he shall have no need of spoil. She will do him good and not evil all the days of her life. She seeketh wool, and flax, and worketh willingly with her hands. She is like the merchants' ships; she bringeth her food from afar. She riseth also while it is yet night, and giveth meat to her household, and a portion to her maidens. She considereth a field, and buyeth it: with the fruit of her hands she planteth a vineyard. She girdeth her loins with strength, and strengtheneth her arms. She perceiveth that her merchandise is good: her candle goeth not out by night. She layeth her hands to the spindle, and her hands hold the distaff. She stretcheth out her hand to the poor; yea, she reacheth forth her hands to the needy. She is not afraid of the snow for her household: for all her household are clothed with scarlet. She maketh herself coverings of tapestry; her clothing is silk and purple. Her husband is known in the gates, when he sitteth among the elders of the land. She maketh fine linen, and selleth it; and delivereth girdles unto the merchant. Strength and honour are her clothing; and she shall rejoice in time to come. She openeth her mouth with wisdom; and in her tongue is the law of kindness. She looketh well to the ways of her household, and eateth not the bread of idleness. Her children arise up, and call her blessed; her husband also, and he praiseth her. Many daughters have done virtuously, but thou excellest them all. Favour is deceitful, and beauty is vain: but a woman that feareth the LORD, she shall be praised. Give her of the fruit of her hands; and let her own works praise her in the gates" (Proverbs 31:10-31).

Look prayerfully and meditatively at those scriptures, and aspire to be a virtuous woman. When you become the virtuous woman God intended you to be, you will have also won your husband and children into the sanctuary of their souls. They will honor you all the days of their lives.

Don't allow the words "submit" and "obey" to be bad words. In the natural order of God, everybody submits to somebody. 1

Corinthians 11:3 reads, "But I would have you know, that the head of every man is Christ; and the head of the woman is the man; and the head of Christ is God."

Now if Jesus has no problem submitting to His Father, then man should count it joy to submit to Jesus. Likewise, wives should count it in their favor to submit to their husbands. Children are taught to submit and obey their parents.

Ladies, the truth is you have the upper hand in this situation, particularly now. In ancient times and during the time Christ walked the earth, a woman had little or no rights. She was regarded as a piece of property. A father could give his daughter to the man of his choice. He might be a moral or an immoral man. He could be good to his wife or he could be mean to her. Women were simply at the mercy of their fathers and husbands. Marriages were more like business deals than holy matrimony.

Today, ladies, your options are clear. You can ask God to steer you toward a man whose life is Christ-centered. Then it's up to you to be patient and not settle for anything less than the kind of man you know God wants for your life. As I mentioned in an earlier chapter, if you want the right one, be the right one. And this comes down to holding high the standard that God has set for you, and not compromising, under any circumstances. I have been married for 25 years, but I want you to know that the same standards my wife held high when we first got married she still holds high today. If I err just the least from those standards, she has no problem reminding me of her expectations. I don't mind this one bit because in essence she is helping me to be the best I can be.

The wedding vows say it is the duty of the man to love, cherish, honor, and protect his woman. Now the way he does this, first and foremost, is to be a Christ-centered man. He is more concerned about church on Sunday than body building on Monday. He is just as excited for you when something great or special happens ... as if it were happening to him. Ladies, when you begin courting, make sure he meets your standards completely. Ladies, you want a spiritual man: one who attends Sunday school–a church-going man. He works on that job and doesn't mind coming home to fix the meal if he needs to. A man of God knows about doing his fair share. It's about doing whatever it takes to keep the home a pleasant and happy place.

One thing I'm learning, the closer I get to God, the closer I get to my wife and family. Being the head of my home means providing the spiritual leadership for my wife and children. It's my duty to bring the spirit of God into the relationship, and I declare that He, the Spirit, will make a woman appreciate the kind of man you are. After all, only a foolish woman abuses a God-fearing man.

As a teenager growing up, I did my playboy number for a while. When I decided to get married, I honestly lost my desire to go to clubs and do the every night socializing. All the dancing I've done since has been at my house with my wife. And we don't try to have a relationship based on what other couples are doing. Each relationship is unique and special. Therefore, it doesn't bother me one bit if several of my buddies never wash dishes or do other chores around their house and I do. Friday nights are reserved for me and my family instead of a night out with "the boys." It doesn't bother me to be called henpecked. My priorities are in order. My allegiance is to my wife and family. I understand that I must lead my family first, and that by example. I must show them the things of God. As a Christ-centered man I realize that my marriage is what I make it. "As Christ is the Head of the Church, the man is the head of his wife."

The key to a marriage hinges on the relationship between husband and wife. This is why unions should not be formed thoughtlessly or irrelevantly; but advisedly and in the fear of God. And the husband and wife must know their responsibilities before they make the commitment.

Finally, on this subject, I want to tell you that you can fulfill your duties when you see Christ as the first object of your affection. Colossians 3:23 reads, "And whatsoever ye do, do it heartily, as to the Lord, and not unto men." Truly this could be a proverb for all to live by: whatever you do, do it as unto the Lord.

Ever wonder what kind of world this could be if every man, woman, boy and girl did what they did as unto the Lord? How happy would a woman be if her man loved her as if she was God's daughter? Ladies, think in terms of your man as the one sent from

God. How much more time would parents invest in their children if they understood that they were God's children? How much more patient would we be on our jobs if the supervisor were Jesus Christ Himself? Thank God I'm learning that when I look at my wife, I just don't see Judy, but I see Judy and Jesus. When I look at my son Joshua, I don't just see Joshua; I see Joshua and Jesus. I'm learning how to do things as unto the Lord. Let me give you just this one final scripture to meditate on. Psalm 127:1 states, "Except the LORD build the house, they labor in vain that build it: except the LORD keep the city, the watchman waketh but in vain."

The story of the three little pigs gives details as to how each pig built their house. One pig built a house with straw, another built with hay, and the last pig built his house with bricks. And as it would be, their enemy, the big bad wolf, came along with the sole purpose of destroying the home to devour them. The moral of the story is to be sure that you build your home on a solid foundation so that the enemy cannot destroy it. This clearly says to me that except the Lord is working in your relationship, helping you to carry out your duties and responsibilities, then your home is sure to be destroyed by the enemy. Keep this in your mind: God always asks us to do things that are in our best interest. Satan, our enemy, always tries to manipulate us to do things to destroy the things that are in our best interest.

I want to challenge you to execute the duties that are before you as husband or wife. Do it unconditionally. Some people are good at holding up their end only if the spouse is working to the same end. That's the ideal situation, but in many instances that simply is not the case. If a marriage is to have a chance at working, then someone must be willing to maintain that high standard that God has set for him or her, and that without exception. The marriage institute is in trouble today because the participants give in too quickly to the temptation of divorce. I am of the opinion and firmly believe that if just one spouse will execute their duties, the marriage is given a real chance of survival. And in a reasonable period of time, a marriage of the highest quality is developed.

CHAPTER FIVE

Be Aware of Family and Friends

What would you think and how would you feel if I told you that a great hindrance in a marriage could be your family and friends? In my twenty plus years of counseling couples with marital problems, I have found that an alarming number of them have problems because of the involvement and interference of family and friends.

If you just pause and think about this subject, you will recount situations where you clearly saw problems in someone's relationship because of a misunderstanding between family members. Have you ever seen two people madly in love but the wife didn't like her mother-in-law? Or the couple seems fine but the in-laws seem to hate each other?

How can you avoid these kinds of problematic family relationships? Let's take a look again at a basic marriage thought in the scriptures: "…For this cause shall a man leave father and mother, and shall cleave to his wife: and they twain shall be one flesh? Wherefore they are no more twain, but one flesh. What therefore God hath joined together, let not man put asunder" (St. Matthew 19:5, 6).

How many times have I listened to couples talk about their marital problems and this statement comes up: "He or she doesn't like my mother." Or I've heard some say, "I love my wife, but I love my mother more because she brought me into this world." In a relationship, there is a spirit that places mother and/or father above the spouse. That is so wrong. Remember that you have left father and mother. "And for this cause [for marriage, for being with your spouse] shall a man leave father and mother, and cleave to his wife."

The People New Testament Commentary says that the bond of husband and wife is stronger than that between children and parents. Don't ever allow your parents or your own sympathy to cause you to think that your greatest love should always be held for your parents. We are sometimes made to feel as if we owe our parents (particularly our mothers) the desires of their hearts, even after we have entered into our relationship with our spouse. We have a tendency to think that no one comes before our mother. This may be true; yet when you get married, your spouse becomes the first love and priority in your life.

I know sometimes, because of love, loyalty and appreciation, we keep our parents on that pedestal. There is nothing wrong with that. Parents have a special place in our hearts, especially if they have been good parents. We should always love and revere our parents. However, parents cannot hold the same place as our spouses. When you get married, you step out and up to another level, and on that plane there is nobody but you, your spouse and the good Lord. This may seem hard to accept but if you think it through, you will conclude that you can't bring family to the level of your relationship with your spouse.

Now because you love them and they love you, parents and other family members can very quickly and easily overshadow your relationship with your spouse. Have you ever heard of the term "interfering family members" and "meddling in-laws?" It does happen. It starts out quite innocently, but the end can be disastrous. Let me share some examples born out of my personal experiences.

How well I remember our first trip coming home for Christmas, when I was in the U.S. Air Force. We were stationed in Denver, Colorado. We had driven straight through (which was at least a thirty-two hour drive). As we approach the city of Calhoun, Georgia (which is only about twenty miles from Rome), we began to talk about where we would stay for the two-week vacation. I remember saying to Judy, "Now when we get to Grandma's house, you just get the baby and go on in the house. I'll get all the luggage and take it to my old room." Her reply was "No, you know we're staying with my mom. She would be so hurt if we didn't stay with her." What she didn't know was that my grandmother (and I, too) would be equally hurt if we didn't stay at her home. True to my word, when we got to my grandmother's house, you could tell that she had made those special provisions to accommodate us. At my grandmother's house we had plenty of room. Her house was a 5-bedroom house. Our baby would have plenty of space to walk around in her walker. But the truth is, I wanted to stay with my grandmother because it was what she wanted and it would be convenient for me. I would be close to her, close to neighborhood friends, close to the church, and the reasons could go on and on. Much to my surprise, it simply was not going to happen that way.

After we had been at my grandma's house for a couple of hours, my wife began to suggest that it was time to go to her mom's house so we could really settle down. We did this without incident, but my grandmother was certainly disappointed, and so was I.

In the car ride to Judy's mom's house, I remember trying to explain to her how there was so much more room where we were, but my wife just wouldn't budge on this issue. We were staying with her mom, end of discussion. That became the pattern for us whenever we came home to Rome for any period of time. We would go by my grandmother's house, but always stay at her mother's home. I never really challenged that because I certainly was not going to sleep away from my wife and children. Later in life, when our family was bigger, we'd have shorter visits and would stay at hotels, but our trip was always planned around the things happening with my wife's family.

Now this leads to a very interesting point that I want to make. Generally speaking, it is the maternal family (the wife's family) who dominates the family relationship. I'm not saying that's good or bad, it's just generally the way things go. As the mother of the family builds the nest of her home, she naturally does it in close proximity to her family. Things just naturally flow in and through the wife's family more so than the husband's family.

That certainly was the case for Judy and me. Our children just seemed to be closer to my wife's family. Her mom and dad, aunts and uncles, and cousins were always in and out of our home, and vice versa. We would do things with my family, I saw to that, but it wasn't the same. I can't explain why but it never really bothered me. Especially when I noticed that was true in most all families that I observed. So guys, you can look for that and don't let that be a problem. My good fortune was and is that I have some very good in-laws. They have always made me feel welcomed into their family.

Now your situation may be entirely different, but whatever the case, learn to go with the flow of things, especially when it comes to your children. In recent years it has been my children who have determined where we spent the most time between our families. They have always wanted to go to their maternal grandmother or to the cousins of the maternal family to spend the night, play, or have lunch. Once we moved back to Rome and settled down, there was another hurdle to jump in our relationship with regard to our extended families. Who do you spend the holidays with?

The first time this occurred was a Fourth of July holiday, and everyone was having a family cookout. Now if you don't live in the same town with your parents or other close relatives, then you may not have a problem with this. But what do you do when both sets of parents invite you to dinner and tell you that dinner is prepared with your family in mind? Sometimes it seems as if your families are jockeying for your attention.

Well, the first time this happened it was a fiasco because we tried going to both places, eating at both places, and greeting friends and relatives at both places. By the end of the day we were not only tired, but also weary from over-eating and grumpy at each other for what we had put ourselves through.

The solution to this was quite easy because it tended to work itself out. In time we simply learned to alternate. We would visit one family for one holiday and visit the other family on the next holiday. Finally, there will come a time when you and your spouse will decide to stay home and enjoy the holidays in your own domain. Believe it or not, everyone adjusts to that. Then there will even come a time when you'll begin to entertain your families at your home—one family at a time. And in time you will have all of them over. The point is you must learn how not to allow your in-laws and their families to control your family. To do it right takes time; but if you work at it, others will learn to respect your family unit and give you the space and respect you need.

There is another way that in-laws and family can create havoc in your family. This happens when you choose to involve them in your feuds. You must be careful as to who you allow into the inner sanctum of your marriage ... the place where your greatest joys and most hurtful sorrows lie. I know you feel the need to tell somebody, but be very careful as to whom you unload your problems.

A very common occurrence is for the wife to tell her mom when her husband is misbehaving or not living up to her expectations. Likewise, the husband goes to his mom or maybe his dad when he feels that his wife is not keeping up her end of the bargain. The problem with this is that you seek support from people who are going to readily see your point of view and be supportive of their child. That's just natural. Of course, there are exceptions to this rule.

When Judy and I had been married about 6 months, a bad storm hit Rome. We lived in a nice apartment and Judy had fixed it up and everything was so neat. The storm, coupled with two to three days of steady rain left our apartment flooded. We roughed and toughed it out. I did all I could to stack furniture, and I rented a dry vacuum machine to dry the carpet. Unfortunately, things did not dry soon enough for Judy. She wanted me to take the carpet out and get it to a cleaner or even consider buying new carpet. Well, I did not like either one of those ideas and I thought it best to simply try to wait it out. I thought to myself, "This time next week everything will be back to normal, and I can save this money that I really don't have anyway."

Judy and I were simply on opposite ends of what we felt needed to be done about this unfortunate situation. When she could not persuade me to get the carpet out of the house, she decided that she was going down to her mother's house until things got better with the carpet and between us. I didn't want her to go, but I was too proud to say anything. There we were, having our first major spat, and she was going home. She went in the bedroom crying about how cold the carpet was to walk on. As she packed a small suitcase of clothes, she also complained that the carpet had an unpleasant odor. She was right on all issues, but I was convinced time would solve our problem.

Then she left and went home to her mom's house. When she got there, something happened that probably changed our lives forever. She told her mom what had happened and how she wanted to stay with her for a couple of days. Much to her surprise and my surprise, her mother refused her. In simple terms, she told her that she was married and that she would not be coming to her house every time a problem arose. Now that might have seemed cruel for a mom to do, but it worked wonders for our marriage at that time. My wife could not go home—she had to come back home to me.

So within the hour she had left, she was back home. And within an hour after that, I had decided to get that carpet out of the apartment. Gee, I can say it now that I was so glad her mom sent her back to me. She didn't take sides; she simply reminded her that her home was with me. When she got back home, I began to hear her reasoning. Because of her mom's objective position we were able to work out our problem. Needless to say, Judy has never left me again.

I'm reminded of another situation where a young lady was mad at her husband because he had come home later than usual a couple of nights in a row. He explained to her that he had tried to call, but each time the line was busy. He had been working late to make some extra money. On the second night that this occurred the wife called her mother sobbing and saying that apparently her husband had found another interest because she simply did not believe he was working extra hours. Her mother did not help this situation because she brought up the fact that she was fairly sure she had seen him in the mall one night last week with a pretty, shorthaired girl. Naturally she said, "I didn't want to tell you but in light of what you've told me, I felt I needed to tell you." Well, this set off a chain of arguments and hurt feelings for days. Accusation here, the silent treatment there, and no one was happy.

When the truth came out, here's what really happened: The wife was having a bad week because it was that time of the month. The guy was indeed working late and had the time sheet and extra money to prove it. The lady with the short hair that the mother saw with her son in-law turned out to be her daughter. The daughter had forgotten to tell her mom that she had gotten her hair cut short. This was a tough week made worse because the wife's mother added fuel to the fire. It's one thing to be supportive of a loved one; but we must remember there are always two sides to every story. We cannot be too quick to draw conclusions. I say again, be careful as to what extent you allow your family members to get involved in your disputes. Sometimes the more people you involve, the more complicated the situation becomes.

One thing I've told people that I've counseled over the years is this: If you are going to involve family members, always talk to your spouse's family first. When things go wrong, don't isolate yourself from his family, seek support from them. After all, they know him. For example, if your husband has had a change in attitude about something, don't go to your mother for support, go to his mother. This must be done tactfully and with love. You might say something like, " John and I are really having some problems right now. I love him so much, how can I get his attention? Will you help me to get through this? I know he values your opinion, and so do I."

Two things are happening with this approach. You are talking to someone who probably knows him best; and you are not telling someone who's first instinct is to turn against him. Maybe, just maybe, his relatives will appreciate your humility and the confidence you put in them. Plus, remember that going to your own family will almost inevitably cause them to respond along family lines. Your family will support you; your spouse's family will naturally support him. When you go to his family instead of yours, you are involving his family. You will need allies from his family. Hopefully they will be positive, objective, and supportive. Therefore, establish and maintain a good and positive relationship with your spouse's family.

As in all of life, friends are important. In fact, friends are invaluable. Some of my best times have been spent on double dates or having another couple over to our house for a barbecue dinner. You certainly need those special people around you to make life complete. You were close friends with your spouse before you carried your relationship to another level.

However, having said all that, I need to mention that friends can also interfere with your marriage. Yes, friends can impact and influence your family in a negative way. For one thing, when you have close friends, sometimes neither of you knows where to draw the line. When I was growing up there was a saying for people in their early twenties who hung out a lot: "We are young, dumb, and having fun." Sometimes this led to petty jealousies and a lack of respect for boundaries.

Judy and I had only been married a year when I joined the Air Force. After my basic training and technical school, I was stationed at Lowry Air Force Base in Denver, Colorado. By chance there were several guys from our hometown stationed just 70 miles south of Denver, in a town called Colorado Springs. One of those guys had at one time been very close to Judy and me. We'll call him David. David had known us since the early days of high school. We played ball together, sang in the community choir together, and on occasion had double dated. David was a good guy. It was only natural that when we got to Denver and heard that he and a few of our other friends were in Colorado Springs that we looked them up.

Now of these guys, I was the only one who had gotten married. Because of this, it was much easier for me to invite them up to spend the weekend with us, as opposed to our going to Colorado Springs. So we would invite a couple of guys to our house for weekend get togethers. Sometimes as many as four extra guys would come up and pile into our modest two bedroom apartment.

It was great at first, seeing friends from home, meeting new people. We all had plenty of money, which meant we basically could do what we wanted to do. Many times these guys would come up and go see Denver. They would simply come back to our home at night for a place to stay. Slowly but surely that began to take its toll on Judy and me. For one thing we did not want to entertain twice a month. Judy was getting tired of cooking those extra meals, and it seemed like she was cooking for an entire army. Then some of the guys would come in real late, two maybe three o'clock in the morning. Sometimes they would have the nerve to bring ladies with them. They would bring strangers that they had met at a dance. They would either finish their party at our house or crash until the morning. Either one of these by now was simply too much. By now I had a part-time job on top of my military duties. That meant some Saturday mornings I would go to work and leave my wife with a house full of company. Some of them we knew very little about.

The straw that broke the camel's back was the Friday I came home early from work, and my wife was sitting outside on the steps crying. When I asked her what was wrong, she told me David had come up for the weekend unannounced. He was in the house eating. When I walked in my living room, there David was, with his shirt off, sitting in my favorite chair, eating my food. I had been there only a few minutes when I witnessed him go into my refrigerator and get him another helping of whatever it was he was eating. At this point I snapped. I told him that the Colorado Springs to Denver party was over. At first, he didn't have a clue as to what I was talking about. When I explained in detail that he and his friends' lifestyles were imposing on my family, his only remarks were, "I thought we were friends."

What is my point? When it comes to friendships in your relationship with your spouse, you have to draw a line. And the best time to do so is early in the relationship. You must protect your boundaries. Entertaining others should be limited, and people staying overnight should be rare. I lost David as a friend because I didn't know how to let him know where our boundaries were. Let's face a fact, friends will take advantage of you if you don't establish some rules about how things work around your house.

I have seen couples split up because of close friendships. The wife may be telling her best friend all the intimacies that take place in her house with her husband. Slowly but surely the best friend develops a fixation on her friend's husband. It happens. Or a young man spends a year courting and dating his soon to be bride. But once they get married, the guy begins to spend more time hanging out with the guys than with the wife he married. She feels all alone and deserted. He wonders why she is always so upset and fussy. Young married people must be careful about who they allow into the sanctuary of their marriage and how often.

I really believe there ought to be a period of time (at least two years) where newly wedded couples spent most of their time together. With the exception of work, the rest of the time should be quality time getting to know each other as married partners. You know when to take those breaks from each other. You come to know when it's time to involve other people in your lives; but for the most part, newlyweds should work long and hard at getting to know each other and being the best of friends.

After that situation at my home with my hometown friends, I never allowed anyone to feel so much at home in my house again. Judy and I started doing more things together. We would do more detailed planning for our weekends and holidays. We became very selfish and protective of the things we were building together. We became and continue to be best friends. Let me close this chapter with a poem that speaks of my relationship with Judy, my wife and my friend.

"I am come into my garden, my sister, my spouse: I have gathered my myrrh with my spice; I have eaten my honeycomb with my honey; I have drunk my wine with my milk: eat, O friends; drink, yea, drink abundantly, O beloved" (Song of Solomon 5:1).

CHAPTER SIX

Family Values

Dr. Lynn Cundiff, the former President of Floyd College here in Rome, became one of my close friends in recent years. He literally transformed this two-year college into a technology community, located on several campuses in the state of Georgia. However, I mention Dr. Cundiff because he and his wife, Glenda, have a tremendous ministry for strengthening marriages. Judy and I were privileged to be a part of a thirteen-week session entitled "Married for Life," taught by the Cundiffs. The book and this program are listed as a reference, and I would encourage couples in any given community to get together and go through this program. It will change your marriage forever.

At one particular session, Dr. Cundiff said these words that shall forever challenge me in my relationship with my family. "Men, when at the end of life we stand before our maker, know that He will not ask us about the job we worked on. He will not ask us what kind of house we lived in or what kind of car we drove. Our God will not be concerned with how much money we made or what offices we held downtown. The first thing our Lord and our God will ask of us is what did you do with the family I gave You?"

I want to talk about family values. How many times have you heard it said, in just about all circles of life, that as the family goes, so goes the rest of the world? This is so true. Therefore, if we can strengthen our families, churches, neighborhoods, and communities, then our cities will be strengthened. We know that there are no perfect families, whether they are royal or peasant; every family is going to have its share of problems. Job 14:1 declares, "Man born of woman is of a few days and full of trouble."

What makes a family a strong family...a good family...one to be emulated...is how it responds to adversity. The behavioral scientists have declared that there are two types of families: the functional family and the dysfunctional family. The functional family has the ability to work together for the common good of the whole family. In other words, members look out for each other in times of adversity. The lines of communication are always open. They are able to do this even if a member of the family is absent; whether dad is in jail or even if mother has died. A functional family has a way of holding it together and getting the desired results that help the whole.

Now a dysfunctional family is just the opposite. Rather than turn to each other, members turn on each other when a crisis develops. They blame each other; they fight each other. Communications can break down, and nobody talks. Sometimes the family members of mom, dad, uncle, and so on are in place, but they just can't get along to the point of resolving problems and issues, when they arise. As a matter of fact, they sometimes make matters worse. The more family members who know about the problem, the more the problem escalates. Dysfunctional families generally have to involve outside help, such as the police, counselors, lawyers, and pastors to help resolve problems. There is absolutely nothing wrong with that. When a family is in trouble, you ought to get help from wherever you can.

I say again, there is no perfect family. However, every family has values of some sort. The problem is too many families have lowered their standards. Children and parents have reversed roles in some families. Vulgarity and cursing is accepted in many families.

Mothers encourage their daughters to take the pill to avoid getting pregnant, thus giving them their approval to have sex. Sometimes fathers look the other way as their sons sell drugs to bring extra income into the family. Young adolescent males are encouraged to participate in criminal activities to be accepted into a gang. Sometimes males are coerced into being immoral as a way of demonstrating their manhood.

Today's families tend to emphasize the importance of self, material gain and success. In days past, the emphasis was on love of family, friends, and faithfulness to God. It is a fact that the family's moral standards of living have fallen; and therefore the moral standards of everything else in our society suffer. And you need only to look at the TV to see exactly what I'm talking about. From Jerry Springer to HBO to cartoons like "South Central," TV is art imitating life. Pretty much what we see on TV is who we are in real life. And even worse, the religious broadcast programs are so mixed and varied that folks who watch religion on TV are more confused than they are helped.

So we are in search of some family values that will truly make a difference in our homes, which will naturally impact everything else that the family touches. Let us continue, then, by looking briefly at the first family in the Bible, Adam and Eve. Let us observe what we can about them.

We learn so many things from Genesis Chapter 4. Adam and Eve, after being banished from Paradise, did what married people do–they settled down and had a family, two sons, Cain and Abel. Keeping in mind everything this family does is a first, we very clearly see a family that has dysfunctional tendencies.

Cain was a tiller of the ground, while Abel a keeper of the sheep. The first religious act of the family was the giving of an offering to the Lord. We see an accepted act by Abel, who brings his first, best and unblemished lambs, and sacrifices them before the Lord. But, we also see a kind of false religion with the sacrifice of the vegetation that Cain offers. The implication is that Cain's sacrifice was not his best because it was not given from his heart. Thus we learn that we cannot approach God with our worship and giving any way we please.

Then, we see another first: Cain gets an attitude, he gets mad with God, and he takes it out on his brother, Abel. Why? Because God accepted Abel's offering and rejected Cain's. Cain is so upset by this that he takes his brother's life. So in the first family we also have the first murder.

Now this situation is a demonstration of just how difficult it can be to hold the family together. The Bible gives no indication, but I wonder where the parents were during this ordeal of Cain and Abel's. Had these two brothers reached the age of accountability and therefore did not involve their parents?

One lesson we learn from the 3rd and 4th Chapters of Genesis is if man does not stay on top of things in his family, the devil will surely take control. It's like the old saying: "Don't let the devil ride. If you let him ride, he'll want to drive." This brings me to the first point that I'd like to make about family values: (1) A family must be functional. In other words, family must be a union for life. That's my definition of family: a unit of people who are loyal to each other forever. A marriage between a man and a woman is a union that makes them one flesh. And their offspring are a continuance of that one flesh. They must look out for each other from start to finish. This is the chief job of husband and wife, mom and dad–hold the family together. It is the parent's responsibility to see to it that their children know they are loved. Children need to feel secure. They must be taught how to take care of themselves. Siblings should look out for each other when parents are not around. In time, they will go out into the world and duplicate what they've seen happen in their family.

There is a scripture that gives that command–Proverbs 22:6: "Train up a child in the way he should go: and when he is old, he will not depart from it." In other words, raise children to have morals, which will develop into virtues, and teach them right from wrong. When they are older, they will draw the line about certain things they do. They are going to experiment and experience things. They're going to try some things that they know they should not try; but in time they will return to their basic teachings and training. In the meantime, parents must pray that curiosity doesn't kill the cat in the process. Believe God that when the dust settles, the basic things they taught them growing up, will fall in place.

A functional family must spend quality time together. Parents must be willing to spend money investing in family oriented things, like Christian education, vacations, and image building things. I worked two jobs to make sure that if my children needed braces for their teeth, they got them. I paid for my son to take karate lessons to learn self-discipline and self-confidence. Invest in your children; it will pay off. Parents must demonstrate much love and patience in order to create a functional family.

It must be said, I'm sad to say, that Adam and Eve might not have been the best parents in the world. When God came to Cain again and asked him where his brother was, Cain's reply was, "I don't know." Then he continued to answer the question by asking a question: "Am I my brother's keeper?" Brothers and sisters, this was not a functional family. Cain did not understand. Perhaps he hadn't been taught or was just resistant to what he had been taught. But he did not want to share the family responsibility of looking out for one another. The responsibility of the functional family, which ensures family values, is a full-time job for both parents.

I want to tell the ladies one more time: you are the nest builders in your home. 1 Timothy 5:14 says, "I will therefore that the younger women marry, bear children, guide the house, give none occasion to the adversary to speak reproachfully." There are no short cuts to the good life God intended for you. Be the lady you were raised to be and build the home you were ordained to make, then your family might stand a chance at being the institution Christ desires it to be.

The next point that I want to raise about family values is this: (2) A family that prays together stays together. I want to encourage you all, wherever you are in your prayer life, begin now to pray as husband and wife; and begin now to pray as a family. This is truly where the man of the house must be the head. I have no doubt in my mind that it is indeed the man's responsibility to make sure that his family members are spiritual in their living. The husband, the father, must sing the old hymns, and pray at the bedside. And if you haven't been doing this all along, your family will look at you strangely. But suffer all that to be so. Call a conference, and start all over again, if you have to. Tell them, this is the new husband, this is the new daddy, and begin to lead them in spiritual things. They may think it's silly, they may laugh, they may think what's the point, they may say it's too late; but men, it's our job to lead our family to Christ and be that spiritual force. Do it until Jesus comes back for you, and God will make your dysfunctional family functional. That's what I love about the Lord, it's never too late. He's always willing to meet you right where you are. Your children may be grown, but you can be a better granddaddy and/or uncle.

So to define the husband's role, I want to give you this: women have to be virtuous, but men have to put off the old man and be a new man who is led of the spirit of God. Look at Ephesians 4:22-32: "That ye put off concerning the former conversation the old man, which is corrupt according to the deceitful lusts; And be renewed in the spirit of your mind; And that ye put on the new man, which after God is created in righteousness and true holiness. Wherefore putting away lying, speak every man truth with his neighbor: for we are members one of another. Be ye angry, and sin not: let not the sun go down upon your wrath: Neither give place to the devil.

"Let him that stole steal no more: but rather let him labour, working with his hands the thing which is good, that he may have to give to him that needeth. Let no corrupt communication proceed out of your mouth, but that which is good to the use of edifying, that it may minister grace unto the hearers. And grieve not the holy Spirit of God, whereby ye are sealed unto the day of redemption. Let all bitterness, and wrath, and anger, and clamour, and evil speaking, be put away from you, with all malice: And be ye kind one to another, tenderhearted, forgiving one another, even as God for Christ's sake hath forgiven you."

You must believe me when I tell you that a man must set the example, set the tone by making his home one of peace, prayer, and happiness. There is nothing wrong with the world, the church, the schoolhouses, or the home that a man ... in the home ... full of the Holy Spirit ... can't change. We need more men filled with the Spirit, willing to be led of God.

Finally, I tell you that family values must include the following: (3) family traditions. Every family ought to look forward to fun, exciting family traditions. A family's traditions help define just who that family is, what they stand for, and what they represent. It is a part of what makes you family. Whether it's celebrating every family member's birthday, having periodic family reunions, planning family picnics, enjoying vacations with family, visiting the cemetery to memorialize loved ones, family storytelling, remembering the family tree and so on, every family ought to have some traditions. Even Jesus instituted the Lord's Supper for the specific purpose of being remembered for what He came into this world to do for us.

A man told a story about a family that had some problems. A man and woman were married and had one son. They raised him to the best of their ability and means. The child was given a good life. They even paid for his college education. But as it would be, he grew to that age of sowing wild oats. He started coming home late at night, cursing and being disrespectful to his mom and dad. His dad grew weary of his son's actions and one night gave him the ultimatum: "Straighten up your act or get out of my house." The son became incensed by such a demand and declared he would leave and not come back.

So he did leave and was gone for years–never coming by, never calling to say hello. This gradually took its toll on the mother. So much so that she got sick unto death. On her sickbed she summoned her husband and made one last request of him. She thanked him for being the good husband and provider that he had been, and asked him to please find her son and bring him back home.

And so he did. He went out all over town, to the clubs, and in the streets. In the ghetto and drug areas he went looking for his son. He went to hotels and to the gambling casinos. Yet, he could not find his son. Finally, he hired a detective and depleted his savings. The detective got word to the son that his mother was sick unto death. Much to the dad's surprise the young man was doing well and making a good life for himself. When he got home, his father met him at the door and asked that they not fuss or make any trouble, for the mother's sake. When he went into the bedroom to see his mother, he embraced her and his mother was so uplifted.

She called for her husband, and the three of them were together again. She took her son's hand and placed it in the palm of her hand; likewise she took her husband's hand and placed it in her palm. As she placed the husband's and the son's hands together, she drew her last breath and said, "It is finished."

And you know that's the same thing that Jesus did for us. When he was on the cross, he took the hand of sinful man and placed it in His hand; then He took His Father's hand and joined it to sinful man's hand, and Jesus said, "It is finished."

The point of this story is when we are joined together with the God that made us, then we as family have a chance to not only survive, but to thrive. A family that prays together stays together. We are family. My household is a smaller family unit of the larger Christian family, and we must look out for each other—in the home, the church and otherwise. How can you love God whom you have not seen, if you don't love your brother whom you see every day. We are family.

CHAPTER SEVEN

The Power of Planning

Proverbs 6:6, 7 states, "Go to the ant, thou sluggard; consider her ways, and be wise: Which having no guide, overseer, or ruler, Provideth her meat in the summer, and gathereth her food in the harvest."

There is an old adage that goes something like this: "Always have two plans. Have a plan A and a plan B just in case plan A fails." I understood the train of thought, but I could never get too far into plan B because it took all my energy and effort to try to get plan A off the ground and running. Besides, careful planning does not always embrace the idea of failing and looking for alternatives.

My friend, colleague and son in the ministry, Rev. R. G. Cole, uses this phrase before his sermons, "Now we are shooting for the moon; however if we don't make it, that's all right as long as we land amongst the stars." So whether you should have a plan A and B, or maybe one well designed plan that will leave you close to your mark, I don't know. But it concerns me that I have observed many people getting married who have not given serious thought to very key issues in their relationship. The idea "… and they lived happily ever after" does not just happen. It requires some careful planning.

I suppose one of the reasons I believe in long courtships is that I think two people should not only make detailed plans for their marriage ceremony, but also at the least some general plans for their married life together. It is a given that there will be good days and troublesome days. Times will come when you simply feel you are spinning your wheels and getting nowhere. All kinds of unwanted, unwarranted, unpredictable occurrences will pop up in your relationship. However, in spite of all the certainties of bumps and nicks in life, there ought to be some definite goals at certain times in your relationship, even if situations and circumstances cause you to alter your goals and the time frame in which you reach them.

For example, you ought to have a plan for how long you want to live in an apartment, as opposed to buying a home. What area of the country do you plan to live in? How long do you plan to live there? How long will you live in your starter home before you move into the home of your dreams? Do you plan to have children? If so, when? What church will you choose for worship? Will you attend his church or hers, or will you find a totally new place to worship? These and other questions like them have to be answered and acted upon.

To further prove my points, consider the importance of careful financial planning in your marriage. Believe it or not, money, or the lack thereof, is a major cause of divorce. This is one of the first things I share with couples I counsel who are about to get married: when it comes to finances, "don't overload yourself." That is to say, don't go and spend and charge for a wedding that will cause you years of grief to pay for and recover from. I learned the hard way, so take this advice from me, "Live within your means."

When Judy and I were married, we were so blessed by people who showered us with gifts and money. We both made good money while we went to school, working at department stores in the afternoons. We really had a good life and stayed well within our means. A year later, I joined the Air Force and we continued to build our lives. We bought our first home and started our family. Judy was often in between jobs because as soon as she had our first child and went back to work, she was pregnant again. That was still not a problem because I often worked a second job and we maintained what I would call an exceptional lifestyle for a young military couple.

The fact is we lived a good life. Slowly but surely that good life depended more and more on credit and credit cards. Credit and credit cards can literally wreck your life if you don't plan the how, when, and why of using them. Just because banks send you credit cards doesn't mean you have to accept them. If you accept them, you don't have to use them. A simple rule for credit cards is to never charge more than you are able to pay off in a 30-day period. There is a thing called interest that makes credit cards an expensive endeavor. Credit card usage should always be short term.

It was also a fact that a military man in a military town could get almost anything he wanted, such as a new car. Even if we didn't need it, I bought it. Clothes, vacations, and other things that were not essentials, but if I could do it, I always thought, why not? For us it was fun. It also got to be a status thing. You know, if the Jones' did something, we had to do something better. Yes, I got caught up in that too. I saw my bills mounting and began to feel the pressure of deadlines; but I always said to myself, "In two weeks I'll be paid again and I'll catch this bill up." This is how we lived, and we did fairly well until the day came that I decided I wanted to get out of the service and go back to the south to live.

Six months before I got out of the service, the reality of my careless spending and lack of planning was about to devastate me. I realized that I had no savings. I was in thousands of dollars worth of debt. I had two children and another child on the way. My wife did not have a job, and in six months I would not have one either. Wow! What a mess, and I had no one to blame but myself.

When we sat down and looked at the reality of our situation, I came close to staying in the military. After all, I knew I would be assured of a paycheck every two weeks. The fact that my wife was not working meant that we could get milk, cheese, and other essentials through the WIC Program. If it were not so serious it would have been laughable. The truth is we were in serious financial trouble. We had a home, new cars, and toys everywhere, but we could not enjoy any of those things for worrying about how to pay for them. And God forbid if anything out of the norm popped up, like sickness requiring prescriptions or engine problems with the car.

We had to make some adjustments in a hurry. The first thing was the most difficult, and that was to send my family home early. While I served out my time, they moved south and lived with relatives so that we could receive their support during our transition. Second, I stopped spending and even sold some things to try to pay off some bills. My biggest help turned out to be a consumer credit counseling program. It was my alternative to bankruptcy, an idea which had crossed my mind more than once. It didn't seem like a bad idea. I would get paid about $550 every two weeks. The problem was I owed $600 - $700 every two weeks. It happened so fast.

I was so embarrassed. Thank God this never put a real strain on my marriage. Judy and I accepted full responsibility for what had happened. We didn't blame each other (like so many people do). We simply did what we had to do to get out of so much debt and on with our lives. It was hard but we survived.

The consumer credit counseling program contacted my creditors and got most of my payments reduced so that I could breathe easier in making those monthly notes. Our house finally sold and we were able to pay a little more on our indebtedness.

When we finally settled down in our new home in Rome it was hard, but that's another story. The point is we learned a valuable lesson: "Get on a budget program, and don't live beyond your means." To this day, we certainly have debts, but I am proud to say that I brought them all under control. Raising our children became a fun thing to do again. We've had some close calls, but we have learned to live within our means.

I know of some other situations where couples did not fair as well. Instead of turning to each other they turned on each other, blaming one another for the financial disaster they found themselves in. I've known of couples who have separated because the wife had been accustomed to getting her hair done on a regular basis. His hobby was tinkering on his car. She loved to go shopping, while he played poker with the boys. He had been accustomed to going to every football game in town on the weekends. She was in the bowling league. Let's face facts, it costs to have fun most of the time. Everyone has hobbies or toys they like to play with. It doesn't seem like much, but when you take on the responsibility of your own home, there's not a lot of room for extra things—unless you've planned carefully. Some people have a hard time giving up those extra things. When they have to choose between hobbies, toys, and marriage, some will opt out of the relationship. That might seem hard to believe, but I have watched it happen with my own eyes.

What is the resolution? Live within your means. In order to do this there must be some time spent on planning how you are going to use your money and learning to use it wisely. I'm not suggesting that what has worked for Judy and me will work for everyone, I am simply speaking from my experiences.

First, we have always shared our money. One bank account–one savings account. What's mine is hers, what's hers is mine. We are a team. Whatever we do together or individually with our money, when it's gone it's gone. If, on occasion, I want to surprise my wife with something, I simply tell her that I am saving some money for a surprise. That doesn't necessarily take away the element of surprise; really, the surprise is strengthened. She knows something is coming, she just doesn't know when or what it's going to be.

Second, we've learned over the years to budget our money. That can be so hard, especially if you've been used to doing just what you've wanted to do as a single person. Or perhaps, like Judy and I, you once had that tendency to get it now and worry about how to pay for it later.

Before you get too far up the road of easy come easy go spending, make sure you have taken care of these basic things. For example, a first priority for every couple ought to be the assurance that the other spouse will be financially stable in the event of an untimely death. Insurance is a must. Unless money is not an issue in your life (that means you have an abundance of it), you must have adequate insurance. Each partner needs health, dental, disability, death, and any other insurance that might meet a need one day. You don't have to have it to the extent that you can't afford it. Insurance premiums can be costly, so start with small amounts and work your way up. In most instances your job will have insurance plans in place when you sign on, and they can also chart you so that your insurance matches your income and lifestyle. Just know that it is imperative that you have insurance. You owe that to your spouse. You owe that to yourself.

This might seem ridiculous, but money can make or break your marriage, so stop and get a grip on your spending. Careful planning to be thrifty now means you can spend more in the future. You will also enjoy life better when you organize and plan your spending, and that's what a budget does. You can find information at the library, bookstores, and on the Internet about budgeting. The easiest way to get started is to simply chart your bills. Write down what your income is and list the bills you pay on a monthly or weekly basis. You will immediately see where you stand. Slowly but surely you will learn to bring about some balance. Hopefully you will learn how to save money, but don't stop there.

In fact, I believe that there are some things you ought to do with your money that are more important than saving it. When I was around thirty years old, I finally had a nice amount of money saved in my retirement plan as a schoolteacher. It was some of my coworkers who helped me to realize that it's one thing to save money, and another thing to invest money. So I started taking some money that I was placing in a simple retirement plan and began to invest it in things that would mean more money for me over time than if I had just left it in a savings account.

My point is plan to save only long enough to begin investing your money in things that will give you the most later on, such as buying a house and renting it out, or buying mutual funds. If you are the aggressive type, you may get involved in the stock market. It is smarter to invest money than to just save money. The interest is almost always higher in investing. Of course some investments are risky, so you want to invest wisely. I'm convinced that if you're not greedy and don't try to get rich overnight, that you'll be fine. Let your investors be your friends or friends of your friends–people who you know well enough to trust with your money and who will make simple, easy to understand, low-risk investments. As your money grows and you learn how investing works, then you can venture out a little further. However you do it, in an honest way make the best of your money.

When you go to buy a car, a home, or any large item that you must pay for with credit, pay close attention to interest rates. Make sure what you're being charged in interest is fair according to the national and state average. These things can be the difference in having enough money for a weekend getaway or a new outfit for the wife. Make every penny count. You can only do that when you plan.

How well I remember when Judy and I had young children, ages two, four, and six. We did not have a lot of money for vacationing, so we learned how to save from one year to the next for vacations. It worked, even if we didn't save a whole lot. One year in the mid

'80s I remember all we saved for a vacation was about $600. That was about $50 a month. As it turned out, we had one of the best vacations I can remember, even if it was only a long weekend at the Marriott Marquis in Atlanta. We took advantage of their affordable weekend rates of $59 per night, and stayed an extra night at the regular rate. My wife had gotten discount coupons for Six Flags one day and White Water Swim Park another. We got general admission tickets to the Braves game. We always stayed on the highest floor of the hotel, so we all could experience looking down and out on the city skyline. Our children always thought that was just the greatest fun. They would make themselves pallets in the floor just so they could look out the window all night. Judy could take $20 and pack a small suitcase full of assorted snacks like fruit, cereals, crackers, and candies.

Atlanta was only an hours drive from Rome, so the cost of travel was really no cost at all. It was not a long vacation, but we often laugh and talk about that kind of vacation because we had so much fun. A lot of our vacations happened because of careful planning. It is amazing how things work better when there is some forethought and work before the actual event.

Finally, I want to give you the spiritual principle for planning, to have money in your life. It's called TITHING, which means giving a tenth of your earnings to your church. The *Easton's Bible Dictionary* says, "The dedication of a tenth to God was recognized as a duty before the time of Moses." Abraham paid tithes to Melchizedek (Genesis 14:20; Hebrews 7:6); and Jacob vowed unto the Lord and said, "Of all that thou shalt give me I will surely give the tenth unto thee." One thing that I have found to be true is that the principle of tithing works. You need only to try it to know for yourself that it works. The Bible is full of spiritual laws and principles that lead us to the highest quality of life there is. The honoring of God with a portion of what He gives us assures us prosperity.

Tithing is an indicator that a person is serious about his or her relationship with God. I heard an old preacher say, "God knows a man's heart by the way he gives, not only to the church, but wherever there is a need." Remember that salvation was based on God's giving, even to the point of giving his Son, who gave his life to redeem mankind. John 3:16 says, "For God so loved the world, that he gave his only begotten Son, that whosoever believeth in him should not perish, but have everlasting life." God is a God of giving and forgiving, which means he is constantly giving for us that we might have abundant, everlasting life. That's how much God loves us. He's always giving, and we can't beat him in giving, no matter how we try. However, for all the blessings he gives us as a matter of principle, and so that His house (the church) might always be taken care of, He commands us to be tithers. And when we respond to His commands, he blesses us; and when we don't, we are cursed.

"For I am the LORD, I change not; therefore ye sons of Jacob are not consumed. Even from the days of your fathers ye are gone away from mine ordinances, and have not kept them. Return unto me, and I will return unto you, saith the LORD of hosts. But ye said, Wherein shall we return? Will a man rob God? Yet ye have robbed me. But ye say, Wherein have we robbed thee? In tithes and offerings. Ye are cursed with a curse: for ye have robbed me, even this whole nation. Bring ye all the tithes into the storehouse, that there may be meat in mine house, and prove me now herewith, saith the LORD of hosts, if I will not open you the windows of heaven, and pour you out a blessing, that there shall not be room enough to receive it" (Malachi 3:6-10).

I cannot explain why it works. It's just God's way, I suppose. When we practice giving a tenth of our earnings (which is what He commands), it's saying to God, "I trust you more than I depend on the money I'm making." It's saying to God, "I love you more than I love money and what it can do for me." If your love for God is greater than money, when you don't have money, God will supply your needs. The tenth of your earnings is what he commands, but in time you'll desire to give more. In time you will give more because you will have more to give. If you are faithful in giving to the things of God, you will always be blessed by God. His blessings upon us are more than silver and gold.

Finally, I want to remind you of a slogan often quoted in the business world, but it should be applied to all of life: "Failure to plan is planning to fail." When you plan something, you are giving some sense of order to your life. Even if your plan(s) fails from time to time, at least it allows you to see what you need to do to get where you want to be. Careful planning requires you to think things through. When you take time to think about your next move, you tend to make sound decisions. Sound decisions will almost always assure you good planning for a better quality of life.

Now make your plans together. Learning strategy and approaches is something husband and wife should do together. Why? Two heads are better than one. You get two perspectives. Encourage each other to see different aspects of a matter so that you can examine all the alternatives as you plan. It also means both spouses learn how to prepare and plan things in the event that something unfortunate should happen to one of the spouses.

Learn how to look at all the issues, points, and circumstances involved, and come up with the best course of action for the entire family. Listen to one another carefully, and come up with the plan that both of you can live with. Then, stick with your plan(s) until you see the end results or you see that you need to rethink or alter your plan. Some things are going to happen in life that we have absolutely no control over; however, we will surely minimize those things when we become managers of our lives through careful planning. Failure to plan is planning to fail.

CHAPTER EIGHT

My Wife's Perspective

On May 4, 1996, the Lovejoy Community Services, Inc., conducted a women's workshop entitled Christian Women in Action for the Lord. One of the presenters for the workshop was my own dear wife, Judy. Her presentation subject was Husband and Wife Relationships. In as much as it was printed in the workshop manual and preserved, I thought it most appropriated to share with you now. These are entirely her thoughts about our marriage four years before I began my work on this book.

How do I begin to tell you, to explain to you how I have had a very happy marriage for 21 years. I must say it is the handiwork of the Lord. To God be the glory for my marriage. Anyone who is married or has been married knows the struggles; how easy it is to fall out with your husband and get mad. Then if you're not careful, you or he will have a tendency to drag the dispute out over a period of days. I have been there too. I am happy to say that those days are far behind me now. God has done a new thing in my relationship with my husband. This is what I want to share with you today.

First, I want to let you know that this presentation is a result of my prayers to God and much time interviewing my husband, the Rev. Carey Ingram. You all know what an inspiration he is to all who interact with him. Carey is special, and I am blessed to have him not only as a Pastor, but as my husband, best friend, confidant, and so much more. So I express this to you not to be bragging, but to let you know that in order to build a good relationship with a man, you've got to make sure you pick a decent man from the start. You have heard it said, "You can't get blood out of a turnip." Likewise, I don't believe just any man will do in a relationship that you want to last over the years. So let me share with you what I can look back on and suggest has made my life with Carey a wonderful experience.

1) Find someone that shares the same ideas about life and living as you. 2 Corinthians 6:14 says, "Be ye not unequally yoked together with unbelievers; for what fellowship hath righteousness with unrighteousness? And what communion hath light with darkness?" This says to me that if I am a church-going woman, I will not go to the club to find a husband. Neither will I base the sacred, spiritual and human needs of a relationship solely on where a man works nor how his body looks. Some men are professionals and make good money, but they spend it all on themselves. A man that looks good is not necessarily good for you. A physically strong, handsome guy may be morally weak and physically abusive.

So how do you choose the right man? Well, the patented Christian answer is, "Wait on the Lord to send you a good man." What does that really mean? To me it means look long and hard before you leap. Take time to know the men in your life. I want to suggest a long courtship (one to three years is not ridiculous) in preparation for a lifetime of marriage. My husband was my boyfriend throughout my high school years and his entire college career. So after about six years of learning each other's ups and downs, moods and attitudes, goals and aspirations, we decided it was right for us to get married.

Couples should not "Shack" or become too intimate before marriage, but a long courtship will help each other to see if they have the same mind and attitude about the direction of their lives.

Perhaps I should have said early on that I know a marriage is lost from day one if the participants are not committed to Christ first. St. Matthew 6:33 says, "Seek ye first the kingdom of God, and his righteousness; and all these things shall be added unto you." God must be first in your life. A couple must put and keep themselves in a position for God to help them when they can't help themselves. There must be a higher authority than you or him, that both will listen to in the time of crisis. If you want a miserable marriage and life, just stay away from church and forsake that real relationship with Christ. There must be evidence of Christ in the marriage. That is to say a marriage should be heavily seasoned with Christlike characteristics. Sister, pray for your man, day and night. A lot of times it's better to tell the Lord about your husband rather than fuss at him. As a Christian lady, don't hesitate to minister to him. That is to say, share scripture with your husband on a regular basis. Highlight scripture, and leave it where he will see it. I just love writing Carey little notes about various things, and those notes are often filled with scriptures. I would like to think that I am helping him without being overbearing.

2) Prioritize your life. "The steps of a good man are ordered by the LORD: and he delighteth in his way" (Psalm 37:23). First there is God, husband, family; and everything else comes next. You would be surprised at how your husband responds to you when he knows beyond any doubt that he is second only to God in your life. (And a man seems not to mind being second to Christ.) If it is a consistent relationship that he sees between you and God, a man admires that in his lady.

Unfortunately, some men don't know where they stand in relationship to their wives. Genesis 2:24 declares, "Therefore shall a man leave his father and his mother, and shall cleave unto his wife: and they shall be one flesh." Sisters, don't put anybody before your husband. Don't ever go home bragging about your boss man on the job or your pastor at the local church or the brother you grew up with. Rarely do I have anything to say about another man to my husband. Most men I discuss with my husband are the ones he brings up in conversations. When I do bring up men to him, it is always basic and simple, and I don't do a lot of praising of other men to my husband. There is no doubt in my husband's mind that he is my champion, my king. Treat a man like he is a champion, someone special to you, and he'll soon begin to act likewise.

3) Christian partners must know and practice the fruit of the Spirit in their marriage. Galatians 5:22 says, "But the fruit of the Spirit is love, joy, peace, long-suffering, gen-

tleness, goodness, faith, meekness, temperance; against such there is no law." Time will not permit me to go into detail on the fruit of the Spirit, but look hard at long-suffering and temperance. To me these two help explain the marriage vows. For better or for worse, in sickness and in health. We are to love, honor, and obey. Just think, that is asking a lot. It requires a lot of giving to make your marriage work. Don't ever forget that much of your marriage is where your love for Christ is also demonstrated. So I believe that sometimes God allows difficulties and troubles in a marriage just so we can learn and practice how to be patient and understanding. Read the first Chapter of James, and see if God has not put you with your husband that together you learn and grow into being the best you can for God, and the best you can for each other.

4) No two people agree on everything all the time, so the next thing that I need to address is what to do when you disagree, fall-out, get upset, get mad or whatever you call it when you and your husband have a disagreement that is not easily resolved. When this happens, and it will, keep the lines of communication open. One of the worst things that can happen in a relationship is to get mad and stop talking–bearing grudges that last over days and days and days. Don't do that. If you are not talking to your husband, guess who does? Yes, Satan takes advantage of you and your partner's silence. Don't ever forget, Satan doesn't want your marriage to work. He knows if he can destroy the relationship between husband and wife, then he is a step closer to destroying the family. Then he can destroy the neighborhood, community, and so on. So remember, behind your disagreements, spats, and misunderstandings is the old devil himself. Learn to fight him and not your husband.

Now the obvious question is, How? Well, keep talking. There

has to be a cooling down period when you get upset, but within a reasonable time (a couple of hours at the most) make your peace with your husband. Ephesians 4:26 declares, "Be ye angry, and sin not: let not the sun go down upon your wrath; neither give place to the devil."

How do you stop the arguments? Look at Proverbs 15:1: "A soft answer turneth away wrath; but grievous words stir up anger." Learn to speak softly and only those things that you really want to say. Here is something I've learned to do, even when I don't always feel I'm at fault. I sometimes take the blame and say, "I'm sorry that this has happened." What's more important in your marriage, who's right on a particular issue or being in fellowship with your husband? I feel it's a mighty good lady who can let go and let God have a situation. You don't have to have the last word in order to have the victory. Remember, you can always let go and trust God to work the problem out for you.

5) Now, I want to finish my thoughts about this subject by reminding you of scriptures that relate to our wedding vows. 1 Corinthians 11:3, 8, 11-12: "But I would have you know that the head of every man is Christ; and the head of the woman is the man; and the head of Christ is God.... For the man is not of the woman, but the woman of the man.... Nevertheless neither is the man without the woman, neither the woman without the man, in the Lord. For as the woman is of the man, even is the man also by the woman; but all things of God."

Without understanding, most women today think it is beneath them to be submissive to their husbands or, as the marriage vows say, to obey your husband." I must confess I used to fight my husband about that very thing. As I said in the beginning, he has grown, I have grown, and together we have an understanding about submission.

First, I clearly understand that my husband is the head of me and our home. He is my leader. I do look to him as the chief, the king of the castle. He then is my protector, my shield, my buffer against the world outside. I understand that it's not about who cooks, irons, or works. He and I share all those things, and neither of us seems to mind sharing chores. It's not about him taking advantage of me or abusing me. He leads in such a way that I don't mind following him. He leads with his family in mind. That's how a Christian man leads.

What is different in our minds? Carey is more concerned with guiding us through getting bills paid and how to meet worldly demands, making sure everyone feels good about decisions we've made. He makes sure we stay on task about our spiritual obligations. My concerns are the same except I deal more in details. As my husband is the head of my life and home, I provide the ingredients for him to work with. That is to say I keep him aware of the things that concern me most about our family. When he responds and allows me to see his plan of action to a given situation, then I help him by reinforcing (at the appropriate times) to him and the children those things he has shared. I offer suggestions that he graciously accepts or rejects; it doesn't matter. What matters is that I suggested. I have learned to be a help mate, and that is very rewarding to me.

So he protects me, I encourage him. He shields me from the world, I provide him with a loving home atmosphere. He gives me security, I know that everything and everybody has to come by him before they get to me. He in turn knows that he has in me a standing invitation to a love, an intimacy, and comfort that only I could give him. When he has battled the world for me and our children, he can come to me and I'll do all I can to heal his wounds. It's a privilege to follow the order of God and submit to my husband.

Just remember, in the 2nd Chapter of Genesis when God made a woman from the man, He did not reach for material from his head. That might lead some women to think in terms of competing with their husband. I don't have to stand shoulder to shoulder in order to love and appreciate my husband. He did not get anything from his back for Him to create me. Therefore, I don't have to walk behind him. Neither did he make me from any substance from his feet for me to walk beneath. No, God raised Adam's arm, reached into his side, and got a rib from Adam in order to create

Eve. This clearly says to me that my place is next to Carey's side; I was created to be his companion. So my husband puts his arm around me and protects me as I walk by his side. I don't get ahead of him, I don't drag behind him, I walk beside him as his helper.

Being a wife is a special place. Just think, a woman is who God gave man to support him in the things that He called him to do. For this, I am richly rewarded.

CHAPTER NINE

Fidelity, the Art of Being Trusted

The *American Heritage Dictionary* defines fidelity as faithfulness to obligations, duties or observances, and loyalty. No one will argue the point that fidelity is a character trait people should demonstrate in all facets of life. Anything worth doing is worth doing to the best of your ability. That requires being dedicated to whatever it is you're doing or whatever it is you're striving to be.

When I was a little boy, I remember Sunday afternoons watching NFL Football on television. All the boys in my neighborhood had favorite teams. I didn't know it then but I realize now that it was the players that gave each team their personality. Johnny Unitas of the Baltimore Colts, Jim Brown of the Cleveland Browns, and Larry Wilson of the St. Louis Cardinals were my favorites. Each team had certain players who somehow gave you a sense of who the teams were. A player changing teams and being traded was not as commonplace as it is today. Today you cannot identify a team by its players because they don't stay with the team very long. There seems to be no loyalty to teams by players. Today, professional sports seems to be about money. Ball clubs are more like money making businesses than teams of fellowship and loyalty. Teams win today by simply buying the most talented players for a period of time.

When we watched the old teams play, we would always go outside and play our own game, rain or shine, snow or sleet. That's how much those players impressed us. They would play hurt. It was obvious that they were not playing just for money. It was about pride and being faithful to fulfill the obligation to the team. It came across in their attitude while playing. It did something to you to watch them play in those days. Some teams would be eliminated from play-off competition; yet you saw them play hard to win every Sunday. They demonstrated a kinship, a sense of belonging that you don't see anymore, in any professional sport.

Strange, but I believe it was watching those Sunday games that I came to understand and appreciate what it means to be loyal. If a relationship between a man and a woman is to be stable and have growth, the couple must be loyal to each other. To me that is the defining word in a marriage, loyalty. Loyalty in marriage is your desire and will to be faithful to that one person you have chosen to walk through this adventure we call life.

Think about this: What could be more heartbreaking than finding out the one person you love unconditionally does not hold the same view toward you? You are dedicating your life to working toward building something special with your spouse. Unfortunately, you find out that your spouse is involved with someone else at a level that should be reserved for your marriage. In other words, what is more hurtful than finding out your spouse has been or is being unfaithful? It breaks the heart and upsets the nerves to the point of permanent damage to the relationship. It sometimes sends emotions into uncontrollable rage. It can leave one feeling inferior. I've known some people to develop a sense of worthlessness because they felt rejected by husband or wife. When infidelity enters into a relationship, it brings hurt and pain. More than that, it brings about distrust–of which the relationship may never recover from.

Generally speaking, it is the husband who often allows his guard to come down, his eyes to roam, and his ego to go unchecked–this leads to infidelity. It must be said that selfishness and arrogance are the reasons behind a man betraying his wife. Men have a tendency to even try to justify their actions with the rationalizations: "That's just a man's way" or "I just can't help myself." When the truth is we often don't want to help ourselves. We are by nature selfish, self-centered, and lustful. The challenge of marriage is to put away that selfish nature and be faithful to our vows.

I want to reinforce that marriage is putting your spouse first.

That is fidelity: putting your spouse's needs first and being faithful to the vows you've made. In very simple terms, married couples are committing to being slaves one to the other. Let me share a scripture that demonstrates what I'm saying: "Let a man so account of us, as of the ministers of Christ, and stewards of the mysteries of God. Moreover it is required in stewards, that a man be found faithful" (1 Corinthians 4:1, 2).

Now this scripture is making reference to the ministers of the Gospel. They are stewards. Stewards were servants who managed the property of their master. In the Bible, Christ is the Master; the church is the Master's house. Stewards are in charge, having the mysteries of God, the revealed knowledge. The knowledge is not their own, but given to them, and must faithfully be dispensed to the household.

Now my point is, just as ministers are stewards of the mysteries of God, the same principle applies to the husband in a relationship. He is given the charge of receiving and implementing the mysteries of God about marriage. This knowledge must be dispensed to his household that the household might be pleasing to the real owner of the marriage, Christ. This only happens when the steward, or in our case the husband, is faithful to the wife.

Nothing can keep a marriage intact or allow for growth and development like faithfulness. In fact, nothing can take the place of faithfulness. It is the one element that must be present in a marriage or, like London Bridge, the marriage is sure to come falling down.

I know beyond a shadow of a doubt that my marriage has lasted because of our faithfulness to each other. Like other couples who work at keeping the relationship strong, Judy and I have our jealous moments. That's right, we sense when others are invading spaces that do not belong to them. When necessary, we air our feelings. Particularly for me as a pastor and a public person, people (male and female) have a tendency to want to possess you and take up a lot of your time. Then, there are those situations that involve my interacting with females where my good intentions could easily be misunderstood.

Likewise, my wife's vocation and position as a pastor's wife keeps her in the public eye. I'm very concerned about the attention and adoration she receives from the opposite sex. So in our relationship there is some jealousy. I'd like to call it godly jealousy.

God is a jealous God. "For thou shalt worship no other god: for the LORD, whose name is Jealous, is a jealous God" (Exodus 34:14). This scripture, and many others like it, makes it clear that God loves us. He cares for us so much and is looking out for our interests. He is bothered and disappointed when His people go in the wrong direction. This often leads to misplaced love for other gods. These are false gods because they are not the one true God. The true and living God knows what's best for us. After all, He created us; He sustains us, so He has a right to be jealous when we don't respond to His love. This jealousy, then, is a good thing because it is born out of love. It is a jealousy that says, "I love you, I'm concerned for your security and well-being in all things. I want you to always look to me to be there for you."

As God is jealous about His creation, so then do we have the right to be jealous of that special person God has put in our lives as husband or wife. Jealousy, then, in its proper place is healthy and wholesome in a relationship between a man and a woman.

I'm honored when my wife says to me, "That lady was staring at you, and I didn't like it. I don't think her motives are pure." When my wife says things like that to me, I have learned that what she's really saying is, "Somebody is invading our space, be careful." I used to get mad at such a statement. Now, I'm honored and I am doing exactly what she says–"being careful." Why? Well, I've learned that most of the time she's right. And when she's not right, I don't lose anything. Women (and men too) can sense when there's something not quite right in another person's intentions with their spouse.

However, even if she's wrong about a new acquaintance or a new church member, I still respect her desire for me to watch my closeness to that person. Why? Because it is my intention to always relieve my wife of any tension or anxiety that someone could ever, in the slightest way, threaten, disrupt, or interfere with our relationship. Remember I told you earlier, "Never allow anything or anyone outside the home to affect your relationship inside the home."

I have heard the conversation where the husband tells his wife, "She is just a friend, and that's all. I refuse to give up my friend because you can't handle the fact that we are just close acquaintances." Well, I submit to that man that any woman who poses a threat to his relationship with his wife is not a friend.

It might just be a silly trick in the mind of your wife that she just can't handle; but if it's real to her, it's real. The sooner you show your spouse your willingness to please them by giving up a friendship, declining a dinner party, or standing with them in a situation that they are not comfortable with, the sooner they will relax in their relationship with you.

Judy and I trust each other, but this is because we've never given each other reasons not to. Even to this day if she suggests to me that I need to be on guard about a person that she feels uneasy about, I respond to that immediately. I try to do this in such a way that she knows very quickly that there's nothing to it, even if it means distancing myself from that person. It has meant completely cutting myself off from some people all together. I want Judy to be assured of my love and loyalty. I shall continually reinforce to her that she is and shall always be my queen.

I shared this information with a friend who is a minister and who was having problems with his wife and her perception of things. His wife was uncomfortable with how close he seemed to be to a lady who was worshipping at the church he pastored. At first he tried to rationalize that if he broke off this innocent relationship with this woman, she might not be saved. I know this preacher was sincere, but his priorities were in the wrong place. I've learned that nothing witnesses to the lost like the example of a loving relationship between a husband and wife, especially a minister and his wife.

So when it comes to another woman in my life, I've learned to follow my wife's lead. If my wife is comfortable with a woman, then I am comfortable with that woman. It's odd, but some of our best friends are women who came into our life through my relationship with them. Judy accepted them and we are all friends. However, there have been other relationships that simply did not work out.

In some instances, there was no apparent reason why my wife didn't feel comfortable with them. When your spouse is put at ease about others around you, your relationship grows in trust and loyalty.

Don't ever forget that perception is reality in the eyes of the beholder. If one spouse has a perception that suggests someone is invading his/her domain, then the other spouse has a responsibility to make adjustments to change that perception.

Most folks say that marriage is give and take; but I want to suggest to you that marriage is about giving and giving. In fact, the vows in the oath of marriage speak in terms of giving: "Who gives this woman to this man?" and "I give thee my troth."

Marriage is about giving. Over the years, I've learned how to give and give and give in my marriage. Guess what? So has my Judy. It is amazing how one spouse will emulate the other, especially if it's good and positive. If you just keep giving and loving and being faithful, your marriage will stabilize.

For me the bottom line is I choose not to have a life outside of my marriage. That makes life outside the marriage empty—but oh, how wonderfully sweet and full the marriage becomes on the inside. Judy and I are one spirit in two bodies. We are soul mates. When she speaks, I speak. When I speak, she speaks. God is my first priority, Judy is my second priority, and everyone else and everything else comes after her. Now I have to work at these priorities, but this is my desire.

People tend to look at us and suggest that we're foolish (to try building such a close relationship). I shall not be swayed by public opinion when it comes to my relationship with my wife. Remember, what people think of your relationship is not nearly as important as what you know about your relationship. If you forget everything I've said in this chapter, remember this: Let nothing and nobody separate you from being faithful to your spouse. Keep that in your heart and mind and your marriage stands a chance to grow and develop. Forget this and your marriage is sure to fail.

Listen to this proverb: "Again, if two lie together, then they have heat: but how can one be warm alone? And if one prevail against him, two shall withstand him; and a threefold cord is not quickly broken" (Ecclesiastes 4:11, 12). This clearly suggests to me that life is not designed for isolation, but companionship.

Let me tell you a little something about the courtship of bald eagles. I read that eagles begin their courtship high on a mountainside. The male eagle spreads his wings around the female eagle, and they drop hundreds of feet to the ground. They do this ritual three times. If the female eagle stays in his wings all three times (until he releases her), they become mates for life. If she fails to trust him and flees from his wings before he releases her, then he looks for another mate. Any wrong move by either could mean death for both of them. So before they commit to marriage, eagles have a way of establishing trust. Like the eagle and many others in the animal kingdom, we are privileged to choose a mate for life. However, we must constantly work at establishing and keeping the trust.

Let me reinforce another important point about fidelity in marriage, mentioned earlier in this writing. One sure way to be faithful to your spouse is to be faithful to your God. I have found it to be utterly impossible to hold fast to the teachings and principles of Christ and be unfaithful in a relationship. The two just don't mix. If you walk close with Christ, you will have the power to be faithful. You will have the strength to fight that lustful nature that arises from time to time. In other words, you're not alone in meeting the challenge of being faithful. The scripture teaches us that there are rewards in faithfulness.

Listen to what the Apostle Paul says about faithfulness to the things of God. "I have fought a good fight, I have finished my course, I have kept the faith: Henceforth there is laid up for me a crown of righteousness, which the Lord, the righteous judge, shall give me at that day: and not to me only, but unto all them also that love his appearing" (2 Timothy 4:7, 8). There are rewards in faithfulness to the things of God. Certainly the marriage institution is one of those special things ordained of God. When we love our spouse in relation to serving God, we are given what we need to be faithful. Faithful service to God will yield faithfulness in the relationship with your spouse.

When you add Christ as the third person of the threefold cord, as mentioned in Ecclesiastes 4:12, then you have the formula for trust and success. Now don't take my word for it, just look around in your neighborhood, look in your community, and look in your church, and see for yourself. Those couples who appear most happy and relaxed in their relationship are Christian in nature.

The words are a cliché for me and oh so meaningful: "Marriage is what you make it." With that in mind I want to suggest that continual counseling is a plus for a marriage. Even after 25 years of marriage, Judy and I are always looking for programs, retreats, and seminars that give us insightful information to help us in our relationship. We have a good marriage–a strong marriage, yet we know there is always room for growth. There is always room for improvement. Sometimes counseling can take place by confiding in another couple that you admire and trust. Sometimes it's going to the bookstore and picking up a book on marriage and sharing it with your spouse. Invite your pastor and his wife over for dinner, and in small talk bring some marriage issues to the conversation. You might find some good, helpful information. There are all kinds of ways to get guidance, help, and encouragement. And believe me, you're going to need it. There is absolutely nothing wrong with ongoing counseling of some sort. The more you learn about each other and relating to each other, the stronger the relationship grows. My relationship with my wife is a top priority. Only my relationship with God comes before her. Therefore, I pursue with all deliberate speed and enthusiasm those things which make our life together strong and happy.

I continue to put the responsibility of the marriage on the husband. It is my job to keep my marriage alive, interesting, and intriguing. At least on a month to month basis, I want to have my wife thinking, "What's next?" Don't be afraid to make suggestions. Don't be afraid to try new and different things to keep your marriage special and refreshing. As long as you keep your life in line with the scripture, go for it. Be spontaneous. Take a mini vacation in the middle of the week. Take up a sport together. Join a club, or take up a hobby. When necessary, get out of a club or drop a hobby. Keep working at making positive changes for the sake of keeping the marriage fresh. Every now and then make a sacrifice.

Give her something that she's always wanted but never thought she'd get. When she sees your effort, she will reciprocate. Marriage is what you make it. So make it something good, pleasant, and sweet. Make it unique, make it yours, and make it fun. Let it be wholesome and endearing. You can give your spouse a sense of fulfillment that can't be compared to any thing. But it starts with being fully committed to her as a person. I promise you, when a woman is confident that she is your one and only, she will emulate that with great intensity.

Keep that old saying true: The grass looks greener on the other side. It may look greener, but make sure that your spouse knows the best place to graze is in his or her own yard (smile).

One final thought about keeping fidelity in marriage: Don't put yourself in a position that could lead you to get in trouble. In other words, don't set yourself up to get messed up. The scripture says it like this: "Flee fornication" (1 Corinthians 6:18). This is a command of God that we must keep in our consciousness. Sex before marriage and/or outside of marriage should be something that you simply commit to not doing for the sake of marriage. It must be something terribly wrong for the scripture to be so forward and blunt to say "flee fornication." I have heard it said that when people engage in sexual activity, it touches every aspect of their lives forever. Therefore people should not engage in this part of life unless they are committed through the marriage institution.

You've heard the saying: "It's so hard to live right, and so easy to do wrong." There is some truth to that, especially if we put ourselves in those compromising situations where we can be tempted. Sometimes it can be as simple as eating lunch with the same person everyday. I mean, some people can handle that, some people can't. It can be flirting: sending signals with body language. You can give some people compliments about their clothes, their hair or body and that triggers something in that person. Now they're walking around with a crush on you, and you don't even know it. Oh, but in time hints are thrown out and before you know it you are in serious trouble. It can all be so innocent at first, but it is sometimes those simple, innocent things that lead to infidelity. Therefore you have to watch carefully the things you say and do when it comes to the opposite sex.

I thank God that my fidelity is in place. But I know that I'm not above temptation. When temptations come, I get myself out of those situations as quick as I can. Another scripture says, "Abstain from all appearance of evil" (1 Thessalonians 5:22).

Over the years I've learned to watch my tongue. You don't have to use flashy words to compliment every pretty girl you see. Sometimes just being a complete gentlemen is the best compliment.

I don't like being alone with women. It happens sometimes, but I don't like it and I try to stay clear of it. When I am going off for engagements, I take my wife with me as much as possible. And I talk about my wife everywhere I go. I know sometimes people get tired of me praising and talking about Judy, but it helps me to stay focused and sends everyone else the message as to who I belong to. Now because Judy is my queen, my soul mate, I say again it doesn't matter to me if other ladies think that I'm a dork or henpecked for being this way.

You can be happy. Your marriage can be something special if only you hold up those very simple principles of fidelity. Keep your vows, keep your word, keep your commitment, and you keep your marriage.

CHAPTER TEN

Marriage is Supposed to be Forever

It was April 8, 2000, and we had just renewed our wedding vows at the Lovejoy Baptist Church. Yes, Judy and I were celebrating 25 wonderful years together. By the grace of God we have shared our lives together, raised our children, and for the most part it has really been a most pleasant and joyful experience. If I had to name the painful or hurtful times, they would be too few to mention. It's strange now, looking back on 25 years of marriage, how good and pleasant it all seems to have been. I am reminded of the scripture in Romans 8:28: "And we know that all things work together for good to them that love God, to them who are the called according to his purpose."

My point is when people commit themselves to marriage and work toward its success, then at every apex, every turn in life, they ought to be able to say that their marriage is worth whatever they've had to do to keep it in the wholesome state intended from the beginning. Yes, there have been some bitter days in my marriage. There were days where we hardly said a word to each other. Some days we did not know what to say. There were times when I've been stubborn as a mule. We've hurt each other, we've cried and sighed, but most of all we survived. We found ways to work through our difficulties. So much so that the bitter days are fewer and fewer as the years go by. I will say that in 25 years, those difficult days would not add up to one year. I'll take that ratio any day. But if the marriage is to last, you will have to address those difficult days with all your body, soul, and spirit.

The evening of our 25 year renewal ceremony, our Pastor's Aid Society sponsored a reception for us. The 200 plus people were treated to every delicious delicacy and assorted hors d'oeuvres one could ask for. The band played a splendid selection of soft music, and at the appropriate time we even danced "the electric slide." It was a great celebration of a lofty apex.

At one point during the festivities, we were exchanging greetings when one young lady, very dear to Judy and me, came by and said, "I am so happy for you two. I have been married for only a couple of years. I hope my marriage will last, but it's so hard." And my reply to her was, "Yes, that's right, marriage is hard." The truth is, marriage should be viewed as one of the great challenges of your life. After you establish a relationship with Christ, if you choose to marry, it should be the next priority of your life. You should put all your energies, effort, genius, and wit into ensuring your marriage will be all that God and you intended it to be.

"Marriage is hard"–each day shall not be like any other, and everyday shall be full of potential troubles. "Man that is born of a woman is of few days, and full of trouble" (Job 14:1). That includes trouble in marriages too. However, there is a response to the troubles of life. Jesus said, "These things I have spoken unto you, that in me ye might have peace. In the world ye shall have tribulation: but be of good cheer; I have overcome the world" (John 16:33).

Holy Matrimony is the oldest institution given to man. It is older than civil government, older than schools of education, yes, even older than the church. Genesis 2:21–24 is where it all begins. The all-wise and powerful God, the creator and sustainer of life, had just completed doing what only He could do–make Himself a world. And you know that this world had the Heavens and the Earth. The Earth was given a sun to light the day, moon and stars to add gleam to the dark nights. He caused the Earth to rotate on an invisible axis, so that we might have a variety of seasons. Summer leads to fall, fall leads to winter. Then after winter comes the spring, and the spring leads to summer. (All these things happened as God ordained them because God is a God of order and every created thing must be in subjection to His way and design.)

Now here comes the land and seas, grass, flowers, green herbs and vegetation for eating. Using my imagination, I believe that then God put his hand down into the seas and stirred the water with his finger. And something started to wiggle, and a one-celled creature began to swim the waters. In the natural order of God's creation, the one-celled creatures doubled in size and began to change in what they were and what they could do.

When God motioned with his hand and one of the fish noticed, he just swam out of the water and walked on dry land; and now there were creeping things evolving into cattle, beasts, oxen, lambs, rams, and rodents. God blew His breath their way, and some went flying through the air. While they were up there, He gave them wings. God ordered everything, and God is a God of order. Now perhaps He did not do it exactly as I described, but my point is God is a God of order; therefore, He ordered the world, things in this world, and mankind to His specific design. Hear the end of my creation account.

God made His crowning creation. From the Earth, He scooped up some dirt, shaped it, and fashioned it until it took on the form of a man. "God caused a deep sleep to fall upon Adam, and he slept: and he took one of his ribs, and closed up the flesh instead thereof; And the rib, which the LORD God had taken from man, made he a woman, and brought her unto the man. And Adam said, This is now bone of my bones, and flesh of my flesh: she shall be called Woman, because she was taken out of Man. Therefore shall a man leave his father and his mother, and shall cleave unto his wife: and they shall be one flesh" (Genesis 2:21-24).

Here we see the first marriage, the first institution ordained by God. The *New Application Bible* says God gave marriage as a gift to Adam and Eve. They were created perfect for each other. Marriage was not just for convenience, nor was it brought about by any culture. It was instituted by God and has three basic aspects: (1) the man leaves his parents and, in a public act, promises himself to his wife; (2) the man and woman are joined together by taking responsibility for each other's welfare and by loving their mate above all others; (3) the two become one flesh in the intimacy and commitment of sexual union, which is reserved for marriage.

In Matthew 19:5-9, the Lord Jesus quotes those same words that were first given by His Father on the subject of marriage. He not only quotes the scripture, but also gives His explanation of what it means. " ... For this cause shall a man leave father and mother, and shall cleave to his wife: and they twain shall be one flesh?

Wherefore they are no more twain, but one flesh. What therefore God hath joined together, let not man put asunder. They say unto him, Why did Moses then command to give a writing of divorcement, and to put her away? He saith unto them, Moses because of the hardness of your hearts suffered you to put away your wives: but from the beginning it was not so. And I say unto you, Whosoever shall put away his wife, except it be for fornication, and shall marry another, committeth adultery: and whoso marrieth her which is put away doth commit adultery" (St. Matthew 19:5-10).

Now the one thing that stands out in this definition of marriage is that it is supposed to be forever; forever being as long as you both shall live on this earth and participate in the adventure we call life. Marriage, from the very beginning and as God intended, does not have options once you enter into it. And the troubled, dying world has its roots in the decay of the institution of marriage. No doubt about it, the institution of marriage is in trouble. Let me share some alarming statistics on marriages in America:

1920-1 divorce in 7 marriages, 1940-1 divorce in 6 marriages
1960-1 divorce in 4 marriages, 1970-1 divorce in 3 marriages
1980-1 divorce in 2 marriages, 1990-9 divorces in 10 marriages

Pastors, preachers, and lay leaders are realizing that we must do much more to promote stability in marriages. In other words, we've got to do more to keep families together. In the Northwest Georgia area (where divorce rates in recent years have been extremely high), ministers and other concerned people have united to bring what is called the "Marriage Savers Program." It is a program designed to train pastors, judges, lawyers, and anyone else who has a heart for helping people hold marriages together. The program trains people how to counsel couples who are going to be married, those who are having marriage difficulties, and blended families (couples who marry for a second time with children from a previous marriage). Further efforts are being made to try to work with all people. Not just the pastors, preachers, or justices of the peace, but the local church congregations are asked to adopt the marriage policy that states no one can be married in the local church unless they are adequately counseled. So if one minister decides not to marry you for a legitimate reason, you just can't go to the next minister and have him perform the ceremony. No, wherever you go in this area, you will have to have extensive marriage counseling.

Some might be thinking these are grave and extreme measures. Perhaps we are forcing our will on people, but we all might observe the signs of the times, before society as we know it is gone forever. What am I saying? In simple terms I'm saying one thing I know that's wrong with the world, the government, our neighbors, our communities, and yes even the church is the decline of the family. And unless we do more to promote and encourage marriages and families, we are a doomed people. I've already been led of God just in this past year not to marry anybody who has not accepted Christ and is not active in the church.

If you come to me and say you want to get married, the first thing I want to know is are you and your would-be spouse saved? If not (unless you can be led to Christ), I will not marry you. Why set people up to fail? Marriage is supposed to be forever.

Now let's look at some things that might aid in holding marriages together. Again, the scripture says, "For this cause shall a man leave father and mother, and shall cleave to his wife: and they twain shall be one flesh? Wherefore they are no more twain, but one flesh. What therefore God hath joined together, let not man put asunder."

Remember I gave you the alarming statistic about 9 of every 10 marriages at the end of the last century ending in divorce. Let me give you an encouraging statistic: At the end of the century only 1 out of every 100 marriages involving devoted Christians ends in divorce. What is the simple lesson here? People who are committed to Christ first, generally are able to live committed lives in a marriage. And that's what every marriage needs today: commitment.

I never shall forget the major in the Air Force who came home one day and found his wife and all the furniture gone. She left a note saying she was leaving him after 29 years. No explanation, no room for reconciliation, just gone. Marriage is supposed to be forever. In other words, keep your promise. If we're not careful, we will become a nation of liars. We'll say anything to get what we want, where we want it, when we want it, and the way we want it; but as soon as the tide turns against us, we are out the door. In our society now a days, everything is political–in the government, in business, in schools, on the job, in the church, and even in marriage.

Most husbands love their wives, but you know if you don't get that card on Valentine's Day, or that gift on your anniversary, then you're in some serious trouble. But there is nothing in the Bible that suggests any one day should take precedence over another when it comes to marriage. Every day is the day to show your wife you love her. Special days are fine; but if you show that unconditional love daily, your wife comes to know that she is special to you every day. If my wife held me hostage for these special commercial days where industries hold society hostage, I would be in trouble. I love my wife, but the politics of special days say I've got to express my love on that day. But marriage and showing love is more than what you give somebody on Valentine's Day.

The scripture says that what God has joined together, let no man put asunder. The marriage vows are the promises that man and woman make to each other. This should be demonstrated on a daily basis, as long as you both shall live, in sickness and in health, for better or for worse, for richer or for poorer, until death do you part. This is the promise you make to each other in the presence of God and witnesses, asking for His divine assistance.

Marriage is supposed to be forever. That's why the marriage vows mention all these unfortunate things that come, like the storms that come in the natural world. Sickness, poverty, misunderstandings, mistakes, regrets, all these things are a part of the relationship, and when you have problems, you are supposed to be committed to staying in the relationship, in spite of those problems.

Some husbands leave their wives if they gain weight. Women leave their husbands if they become bald. I know a story of a man who left his wife because she developed breast cancer and had to have a mastectomy. Can you imagine how much in love a man must be with himself to leave his wife because her sickness leaves her with a scar?

There is a woman who left her man when he lost his well paying job and couldn't find work fast enough to keep the new car he had bought her. In other words, she loved the car more than she loved her husband. Marriage is supposed to be forever, and we must keep our promise.

The Bible gives only one exception. When one spouse is guilty of adultery, that is grounds for divorce. Even then, it's not what God really wants. Any time a marriage in trouble can be reconciled, that should be the goal. That's what Christ was referring to in the scripture. "They say unto him, Why did Moses then command to give a writing of divorcement, and to put her away? He saith unto them, Moses because of the hardness of your hearts suffered you to put away your wives: but from the beginning it was not so. And I say unto you, Whosoever shall put away his wife, except it be for fornication, and shall marry another, committeth adultery: and whoso marrieth her which is put away doth commit adultery" (St. Matthew 19:7-9).

In other words, Moses suffered divorce (Deuteronomy 24:1-4) as a way to protect a woman's civil rights in those days. A man could not just cast her away. He had to have some papers drawn up explaining why he felt this woman was no longer suitable for him, giving her an opportunity to get on with her life. And this was only to be done if a spouse had been unfaithful, and they could not reconcile their relationship.

So divorce is not what God intends, it is simply what he tolerates. Well, Mr. Writer, are you trying to tell me I should let that husband curse me? Should I let my man beat on me? Do you think I'm going to let a man be involved with other women and bring diseases to my bed? No, no, no, no! God does not desire any man or woman to stay in an abusive relationship. So the obvious question is, What are you to do? Well, as I've stated in earlier chapters, be careful about getting into bad relationships. "Be ye not unequally yoked together with unbelievers: for what fellowship hath righteousness with unrighteousness? and what communion hath light with darkness?" (2 Corinthians 6:14). We need to know that an ounce of prevention is worth a pound of cure.

I used to hear the story of the man who found a rattlesnake in the dead of winter. It was almost dead and in the middle of a trail. The man put the snake in his bosom and took it home. Still in his bosom, he fed it and nurtured it. As soon as it felt better, the snake bit the man. The man ask the rattlesnake, "Mr. Rattlesnake, why did you bite me, after all the things I've done for you?" The rattlesnake's only reply was, "You knew I was a snake when you put me in your bosom." Many marriages are in trouble from the start because we don't choose the right spouse. We don't involve God in the process. We marry folks based on looks or because they dance so well. Then you get him/her home and he/she dances on your head. When you are picking a partner for life, you've got to take your time and be very selective. I am one of those old fashioned kind of guys who believes that parents ought to be involved in the selection of a husband or wife for their children. You can decide to what extent, because ultimately the decision is yours.

Parents have raised their children and invested so much in their children's lives. Good parents should be supportive in helping their children decide about someone special to spend their lives with.

Then when you get married, you've got to keep your third partner involved in your relationship, because the third partner (Jesus Christ) can save the whole family. Marriage is supposed to be forever. "And unto the married I command, yet not I, but the Lord, Let not the wife depart from her husband: But and if she depart, let her remain unmarried, or be reconciled to her husband: and let not the husband put away his wife. But to the rest speak I, not the Lord: If any brother hath a wife that believeth not, and she be pleased to dwell with him, let him not put her away. And the woman which hath an husband that believeth not, and if he be pleased to dwell with her, let her not leave him. For the unbelieving husband is sanctified by the wife, and the unbelieving wife is sanctified by the husband" (1 Corinthians 7:10-19).

Marriage is supposed to be forever. Let me share some final thoughts that may help you in keeping your marriage in that sacred and special place in your heart and mind.

Know that marriage is give and give. If couples will dedicate themselves to being givers and not takers, then their marriages have a better chance of surviving almost anything. You have to learn to love your spouse in spite of his or her faults and failings. You must not only love because of, but also in spite of. Love when it's going good, and love when it's not good at all. Marriage is about giving, not taking.

You've got to want your marriage to work. One of my favorite sayings to all those I counsel in marriage sessions is, "Your marriage is what you make it." I love to tell couples it's you and your spouse against the world. Let nothing on the outside of your home negatively affect what goes on inside the home. Think in these terms: All you've got is you and your spouse. No one on earth comes before my loyalty to my spouse. Even your children will grow up and move on, so keep them second in the chain of the love relationship. Spouses should try to spoil each other as much and as often as possible. After all, you are husband and wife, you are all you've got.

Remember, a family that prays together stays together. Your marriage will last if your third partner is Christ and if you talk to Him daily. Include Him in all your plans. Pray consistently with your spouse. I strongly suggest that you pray at least two times a day together. There is power in prayer. God blesses mightily those couples who spend time in prayer acknowledging Him. Proverbs 3:6 says, "In all thy ways acknowledge Him and He shall direct thy paths."

Finally, hold on! Through the storms and through the rain, hold on. When trouble arises, don't turn on each other, turn to each other and hold on. Don't just hold on, but hold each other while you hold on. There is still something very special about the power of eye contact and touch. Marriage is about not giving up and not giving in, it's about holding on until the necessary changes are made for better days. When two people really love each other and work at their relationship, you can rest assured that better days are ahead.

ABOUT THE AUTHOR

Carey N. Ingram is a native of Rome, Georgia. It was always his desire to give back to the community where he grew up. He is certainly doing that. A minister for over 23 years, he is in his 13th year as Pastor of the Lovejoy Baptist Church.

He is involved in various local community activities. He is a disc jockey whose Gospel program, "The Upper Room Experience," has one of the highest ratings in the region. He has received the prestigious "Teacher of the Year" for Northwest Georgia Education Program in 1987. He is a member of the "Leadership Rome Alumni" for Northwest Georgia after having successfully completed the leadership development course of the Greater Rome Chamber of Commerce, in 1989. In the year 2000, Rev. Ingram was one of six named as a recipient of the "Heart of the Community Award." This award recognizes the volunteer services of those who help make Rome that special place to live.

In the summertime Rev. Ingram lends his expertise to NYSP (National Youth Sports Program), where he has served as the liaison officer for more than a decade. He's the founder of the Lovejoy Community Services, Inc., the service branch of the church; and a member of the 100 Black Men of Rome, Inc., that mentors children in middle school grades. Rev. Ingram is on the Rome Boys and Girls Club board, AIDS Resource Council, Good Neighbor Ministry, and Rome and Floyd County Jail Ministry.

Rev. Ingram received a Bachelor of Arts degree in Communications from Shorter College in 1976; served a tour of duty in the U.S. Air Force, 1976-1980; attended the ITC Seminary in Atlanta, Georgia, 1980-1982; and received a Master's of Education degree from West Georgia College in 1987. As an ordained minister, he is the first vice president of the Northwest Georgia Association, and a member of the Georgia State Convention and the National Baptist Convention, USA, Inc.

Rev. Ingram has been married to the former Judy Slack for over 26 years, and they have three children: Tashia, Joshua and Michelle.